What's Up with Boys?

Everything You Need to Know about Guys

CRYSTAL KIRGISS

What's Up with Boys?

Everything You Need to Know about Guys

CRYSTAL KIRGISS

ZONDERVAN™

WWW.ZONDERVAN.COM

invert

www.invertbooks.com

What's Up with Boys
Copyright © 2004 by Youth Specialties

Youth Specialties Books, 300 South Pierce Street, El Cajon, CA 92020, are
published by Zondervan, 5300 Patterson Avenue SE, Grand Rapids, MI 49530

Library of Congress Cataloging-in-Publication Data

Kirgiss, Crystal.
  What's up with boys? : everything you need to know about guys / by
Crystal Kirgiss.
      p. cm.
  ISBN 0-310-25489-2 (softcover)
  1. Girls--Religious life. 2. Man-woman relationships--Religious
aspects--Christianity. I. Title.
  BV4551.3.K57 2004
  248.8'33--dc22

                                                                2004008754

Editorial direction by Rick Marschall
Art direction by Jay Howver
Editing by Janie Wilkerson
Proofreading by Joanne Heim
Cover design by Burnkit
Interior design by Sarah Jongsma
Printed in the United States of America

06 07 08 09 / DC / 10 9 8 7 6 5

Thanks to . . .

—Camille Miller, Tyler Thigpin, and the students of Grace Fellowship Church;

—Brandi Loope-Pemberton, Jason Stevenson, Mary Jenkins, Jason Mayhall, and the students of Stonebriar Church;

—John Coler and the students of Hope Lutheran Church;

—Dave Gruthusen and the students of Arlington Heights Evangelical Free Church;

—the choir students of Detroit Lakes High School;

—and the Senior Knights of the Round Table . . .
        Kyle Anderson
        Nathan Benson
        Ryan Bridgeman
        Will Frank
        Mike Frankberg
        Mark Kozitka
        Sam Mosher
        Adam Schmidt

. . . for your honesty, openness, insight, and humor.

To the guys in my life . . .
Mark, Tyler, Tory, and Tate

Contents

P.S.

I'm a big fan of the P.S. When I write e-mails or letters, I often get to the end and realize I've forgotten to include an important piece of information. Or I think of one last thing I want to say before hitting the "send" button or before sealing the envelope. This P.S. is at the front of this book because it has those last-minute important things that you must know, but you must know them *before* you read anything else. Lots of people put this kind of stuff in an introduction, but since so many people skip introductions, I'm going to put it in a P.S. and hope that people are curious enough to read it before skipping to chapter 1.

First, a little about me. I have three teenage sons. I've been married to Mark Kirgiss for almost 20 years. Mark works for Young Life, an organization that shares the gospel with teenagers, so in addition to our own three teenagers there are hundreds more with whom we spend our time. I work part-time at the local high school helping with the choirs and the musicals, so not only do I hang out with teenagers outside of school, I also hang out with them inside of school.

I'm female (obviously), and I think females are awesome. We have been designed amazingly by God the creator, and I've never wished that I'd been born a boy instead.

I am surrounded by males. My husband, my sons, and our pet bird outnumber me in a huge way. I feel the same way about males as I do about females. They are awesome. They've been designed amazingly by God the creator, and I hope that guys never wish they'd been born girls instead.

I'm a big fan of girls. I'm a big fan of guys. And that's why this book exists . . . because I want all girls to be fans of guys. I think if girls understood guys a little bit better, that would be possible.

As you read this book, be aware of the fact that it often speaks in general terms. In other words, most of these things are true for most guys and girls, but not all of these things are true for all guys and girls.

Humans are unique individuals. No two are alike. But there are some things that are generally true for most girls and other things that are generally true for most guys. Throughout the chapters don't ignore the parts that don't seem to apply to you because they *will* apply to someone you know. And don't judge people by how closely they fit the typical male/female profile. For example, a lot of guys excel at sports. But some don't. It would be a grave mistake

Girls wear dresses and boys wear outfits.
Bryssa, age 4

for you to view the non-athletic guys as somehow less male than the athletic guys. In the same way, a lot of girls are talkative. They talk with their friends at every available opportunity. But some don't. It you know a girl—or if you yourself—aren't very talkative, don't assume that your brain is somehow less female than those who are ultrachatty.

Every person is made just the way God intended him or her to be. No guy is exactly like any other guy. No girl is exactly like any other girl. But in general most guys have some common characteristics, and in general most girls have some common characteristics.

So flip the page and start reading about why boys are the way they are. You'll see that it's not supercomplicated, but neither is it as simple as that old saying, "Boys will be boys."

—Crystal

Boys like to get married.
Lauren, age 3

LIST THREE THINGS
YOU DON'T UNDERSTAND
ABOUT GUYS

Why they don't like to bathe. Why they don't like
to shave. Why they say they worry about their looks
but don't do any of the above.
—Liz, 15

How they can get ready in two minutes and look great.
Why they're not attached to their friends like girls are.
Why their lives revolve around cars.
—Ruby, 17

Why they know NOTHING about girls.
Why they act like tough guys.
Why they don't tell people how they feel.
—Sarah, 15

Why they think just because they can grow facial hair,
they should. Their ability to eat everything in the world
and not gain weight. Why they think just because I'm a girl
I can't be a marksman on the rifle range.
—Kelley, 17

How they can always do better than girls.
How they are allowed to get mad at girls
but not vice-versa. How they care about something
for a good five minutes, tops.
—Melissa, 16

Why they beat each other up and then
the next minute they're best friends.
Why they have to have farting contests
to impress each other. Why they drive
with their seat reclined way back.
—Amy, 16

Why they act so immature. Why they belch in public.
Why they are so rude sometimes.
—Samantha, 16

Why they are hairy. Why they can't be nicer.
Why they are so fascinated with getting dirty.
—Kari, 16

Why they don't look at you when they talk.
Why they grunt. Why they won't clean up.
—Paula, 16

How they can get ready in three minutes.
Why they always laugh at girls.
Why they always hit each other.
—Brittany, 16

Why they always have to win. How they generally
love danger. Why they don't just say what they're feeling.
—Cherline, 16

Why they always hit each other. Why they're always mean
to each other. Why they constantly goof off.
—Rose, 15

Why they are strange.
Why they are so much taller than me.
Why they don't express their feelings.
—Marie, 17

The way they are indecisive. They way they laugh
when nothing is funny. The way they complain about girls.
—Jennifer, 16

Why they always make noises. Why they freak out over
emotional stuff. Why they talk about weird things.
—Jessica, 16

Why they can't dress themselves neatly.
Why they spend hours washing their cars but not their hair.
Why they don't ever have an opinion.
—Lisa, 16

You think they like you, but the next day
they're like "whatever." Baggy Skater boy pants.
How they're always worrying about their hair.
—Lizzy, 11

The way they act. They way they dress.
They way they eat.
—Allie, 12

Chapter 1

The T-Shirt

It all started with a T-shirt . . .

A few years ago I was hanging out in the choir room at the high school where I work part-time. A group of girls and I were eating our lunches, talking about the day, complimenting Annie on her cool toenail polish, admiring Kayla's pink-streaked hair dye, and congratulating Amy on making the girls' varsity hockey team when in walked Erin, wearing a blazing pink T-shirt. Across the front it read,

"BOYS ARE STUPID . . . THROW ROCKS AT THEM."

Everyone laughed at her shirt and started making comments like,

"Ohmigosh, that is soooo true!"

"Where did you buy that shirt? I want one too!"

Boys like to joke a lot.
Tanner, age 7

"Whoever designed that shirt must know my brother."

"Boys aren't just stupid. They're stupider than stupid."

"What's the problem with boys, anyway?! They are so annoying."

"I wish I'd had some rocks to throw at Travis during algebra this morning."

Before long the comments had turned into a heated conversation about what boys are like, how they act, the things they do, and the stuff they say. All in all the girls pretty much ripped the entire male population at their high school to shreds. They had a million complaints and almost no compliments. In the end the general consensus was that Erin's T-shirt spoke the truth, and that even if it wouldn't be very nice for the girls to actually throw rocks at boys, it sure was fun imagining what it would be like if they did.

I don't want you to get the wrong impression about these girls. They're not violent. They're not delinquents. They don't spend their time in the school detention center. They don't walk through the school halls looking for someone to pick a fight with. They've never had to serve an in-school-suspension for anything more serious than having too many tardies in one class. And I'm quite sure that they're not in the habit of throwing rocks at anyone . . . not even boys.

They're nice, decent, friendly, typical teenage girls.

And at one time or another most nice, decent, friendly, typical teenage girls find themselves becoming very frustrated, confused, and annoyed by typical teenage guys.

That's probably why you're reading this book—to help you understand guys better.

Girls like to play house.
Lauren, age 5

That day in the high school choir room, while all those girls were voicing their opinions about boys, I started thinking about some things.

First, if a boy wore a T-shirt that said "GIRLS ARE STUPID . . . THROW ROCKS AT THEM," there'd be a major scene. The principal would probably tell him he couldn't wear such a sexist shirt. The girls would all gang up on him and start lecturing him about being rude and mean. The female teachers would pull him aside and gently talk to him about how hurtful and unkind and insensitive he was being to females. And the boy's mother would probably send him to his room for a month with no dinner. Why, then, wasn't Erin treated the same way? Is it possible that in today's world there's some kind of double standard that says it's okay for girls to voice their negative opinions about boys but not the other way around?

Second, since I have three teenage sons whom I happen to love dearly, even when they drive me nuts, I happen to think that teen guys are okay. Yes, they're hard to understand sometimes. Yes, they're annoying sometimes. Yes, they can be weird, different, and completely wacko sometimes. But isn't the same thing true of teen girls? Aren't we all, girls and guys alike, confusing, mysterious, and hard to figure out sometimes?

Third, it's clear that girls and guys are different (and not just in the obvious physical ways). If they weren't different, there wouldn't be so much frustration, so much misunderstanding, so much teasing and ridicule and making-fun. There wouldn't be half as many jokes in all the comic strips, television shows and movies. There wouldn't be so many different magazines. There wouldn't be words like *he*, *she*,

Boys behave much worse than girls.
Madeleine, age 8

his, and *hers*. There wouldn't be a guys' section and a girls' section at Old Navy.

There wouldn't be T-shirts that said,

"BOYS ARE STUPID . . . THROW ROCKS AT THEM."

The history of how males and females relate to one another goes way back to the very beginning of time, to the moment in creation when God made a man and then made a woman. He didn't make a man and then another man. He didn't make a woman and then another woman.

He made a man. And then he made a woman. And they were very different right from the start. First, they were different because each was a unique individual. Maybe one liked strawberries, the other grapes. One might have preferred cats, the other dogs. Maybe he liked sunsets and she liked sunrises. Who knows? But certainly, they had personalities that were distinct and uniquely their own. Otherwise, why would God have created both of them? If they were intended to be the same, he could have created the man and then simply cloned him.

Second, since one was a male and one a female, they were different by virtue of their gender.

Gender is a hot topic in today's world. There are arguments about what it is, how it develops, and how it affects individuals. Scientists, anthropologists, and psychologists have all kinds of opinions about the subject. Some believe that gender is a real issue. Others believe that gender is simply a man-made topic. Some believe gender is part of a person from the time of birth (nature) while others believe it is determined by how a child is taught and raised (nurture).

Girls cry more than boys.
Eden, age 4

So let's start by defining gender. Some people may define it differently, but for the sake of this book we'll agree that human gender is a classification based on whether a person is male or female.

If something has no gender or no defining characteristics, it is generic. That term is used mostly at the grocery store when we talk about generic brands, those items that don't come from a big-name, well-known, quality company. Name-brand items are often referred to as "the real thing," and many people, especially kids, claim that generic brands don't taste as good as the real thing. In some cases, like Cheerios® and Lucky Charms® I'd have to agree.

The same is true of human beings. God made human beings with different genders because it gives the world more flavor, more variety, more taste, and more zing. In his book *Wild at Heart*, John Eldredge writes, "God doesn't make generic people; he makes something very distinct—a man or a woman. In other words, there is a masculine heart and a feminine heart, which in their own ways reflect or portray to the world God's heart."

I agree with him. Males and females are distinct. Masculine and feminine traits are distinct. And they were both equally created in the image of God.

That's not to say that males have only masculine traits and females have only feminine traits. Since both of them reflect the image of God, then both of them are present in human beings. But males tend to have more masculine traits, and women tend to have more feminine traits.

Initially, we define a person's gender simply by the reproductive system. When a baby is born, the first question people ask is almost always, "Is it a boy or a girl?"

Girls don't like to get their skirts dirty.
Tanner, age 7

And how does the doctor or the parents know the answer to the question? Simple: by looking between the baby's legs. End of discussion.

But gender is so much more than that. If we could see inside a baby's head at birth to see its brain, we'd probably be able to tell whether the baby was a boy or a girl. Why? Because male and female brains are different, even at birth. If we measured levels of hormones at birth, we'd be able to tell whether the baby was a boy or a girl. Why? Because male and female hormone levels are different, even at birth. You see, being male or female involves so much more than sexual organs. It involves the entire being . . . how we think, how we develop physically, how we communicate, how we react, and how we behave. You are a female through and through. That's how God designed you and made you. And guys are males through and through. That's how God designed them and made them.

For a very long time, people recognized that there were differences between the two sexes (we'll talk about the differences later on). But they didn't stop there. They went on to say that, because of the differences, only men could and should do certain things, like becoming doctors, and only women could and should do certain things, like being teachers.

The people who believed this were wrong. Different or not, there is really only one thing that a woman is incapable of doing—being a dad. And there is really only one thing that a man is incapable of doing—being a mom.

About 60 years ago the tide shifted. People started saying that men and women weren't different at all (except for their reproductive organs). They went on to say that since

Boys like to be rough.
Lauren, age 5

they weren't different, then not only _could_ men and women do the same things, but they also _should_ do the same things. In other words, there should be an equal number of male and female soldiers, an equal number of female and male inventors, an equal amount of absolutely everything.

The people who believed this were wrong again. Just because men and women are capable of being doctors, lawyers, teachers, artists, and everything else doesn't mean that they are the same.

I think it's time for us to find some middle ground, don't you? I don't want to live in a world that tells me, "You can't do this because you're a female." Nor do I want to live in a world that tells me, "You must do this because you're a female." I want to be the best "me" that I can be.

And I truly believe that guys want the same thing. They don't want to be told that, because they're male, they can't cry. Nor do they want to be told that because they're male, they must be athletic and competitive all the time.

Each guy, just like each girl, is a uniquely designed and created individual. Each guy, just like each girl, has certain characteristics that are created in the image of God. Each guy, just like each girl, is deeply loved by Jesus Christ.

Guys and girls are not only unique as individuals. They are also unique as a whole group, meaning that guys as a whole are different in many ways from girls as a whole. And that's where gender comes in again. Male and female. Both created by God. Both loved by God. Both pursued by God.

And both different from each other.

Even very young children know this is true. Here are two lists, one written by a four-year-old boy and the other by a four-year-old girl, of the top 10 ways that boys and girls are different. Both of these children are from families that believe in giving their children all kinds of opportunities. The little boy was allowed to play with dolls if he wanted. The little girl was allowed to play with trucks if she wanted. They weren't told they could only do certain things because of being a boy or girl. Neither one had been taught that boys are one way and girls are another.

They were just two typical four-year-olds who had observed certain things about boys and girls in their short lives.

TOP 10 WAYS
BOYS ARE DIFFERENT FROM GIRLS

Compiled by Linni, age four, Atlanta

1. Boys like to play with trucks more than girls.
2. Boys like to eat more than girls.
3. Boys like dinosaurs more than girls.
4. Boys are bigger than girls.
5. Boys have shorter hair than girls.
6. Boys don't wear dresses.
7. Boys don't wear their coats when it's cold outside.
8. Boys are taller than girls.
9. Boys can be daddies, but girls can't.
10. Boys have tails. [Think about it for a second and you'll understand!]

Boys like to get dirty and stay that way.
Joshua, age 10

TOP 10 WAYS GIRLS ARE DIFFERENT FROM BOYS

Compiled by Austen, age four, San Diego

1. Girls wear dresses.
2. Boys wear underwear; girls wear panties.
3. Girls leave the seat down.
4. Girls have long hair.
5. Girls don't play baseball.
6. Girls don't have pee-pees.
7. Daddies have hairy bodies.
8. Girls like dolls.
9. Mommies use makeup instead of shaving cream.
10. Girls scream; boys roar.

Not only are their lists different, but the way they created their lists was also different. Linni sat at her kitchen table coloring a picture while dictating her list to her mom. It only took her a few minutes. Austen, on the other hand, needed almost four days to put his list together. He was too busy doing other things, like running through the house with his cars and trucks. When he finally got to number four on his list, he ran past his mom while making loud engine noises and said, "Mom, can't you just do it for me?"

So were Linni and Austen brainwashed by the world to believe that boys and girls are different? Or were they honest and childlike enough to recognize and admit what most of us already know—that boys and girls are, in fact, different?

I don't think they were brainwashed. I think they're smart. And I think they are lucky to have parents who let them be who they are. Austen likes trucks. His mom and dad never said, "Now, Austen, in order to be a well-rounded,

Boys like to wrestle.
Matthew, age 7

sensitive male you must spend as much time playing with dolls as with trucks." Linni likes to color. Her mom and dad never said, "Now, Linni, in order to be a strong, assertive female you must spend as much time jumping on the furniture as you do coloring." On the other hand if Austen did like to play with dolls, his mom and dad wouldn't stop him, and if Linni liked jumping on the furniture, her mom and dad wouldn't stop her. Wait . . . I take that back. They probably would stop her. But if she liked playing with trucks, they wouldn't stop her.

All of this is to say that the reason you're reading this book is not because guys are just like you. If they were, you wouldn't have any questions about them. You're reading this book because most guys aren't like you, and as a result you're confused, bothered, and even annoyed by them. At the same time, you want to understand them better rather than go through life being confused, bothered, and annoyed.

After surveying hundreds of teens from across the country, I found that most girls have the same questions about guys. They are—

Why do guys act so tough and macho?

Why are guys so competitive?

Why do guys act one way around girls and another around their friends?

Why do guys act so immature?

Why won't guys talk about stuff?

Why won't guys show emotions?

What's the big deal with body noises?

Why are guys so obsessed with sex?

Why do guys always have to be right and be in charge?

Why are guys so insensitive?

Did you notice that each of those questions has a slightly negative tone? I don't think the girls necessarily intended it to be that way. But in today's world it's pretty common for females to lump all males into a group and then refer to them as childish, gross, insensitive, macho, and disgusting jerks. That's unfortunate, both for the girls and the guys. For the guys because it reduces them to some kind of sub-human, rude beasts. For the girls, because it doesn't help them look beyond a guy's immediate and still-developing character to the man that lies inside, waiting to emerge.

Girls, the fact is that guys often do act immature—and gross, and silly, and all those other things that were listed on the survey. But they are still awesome, amazing, and wondrous creations of God.

By the way, the guys' surveys included a long list of things that they don't understand about girls. They are—

Why do girls talk all the time?

Why do girls worry so much about how they look?

Why do girls always talk about how fat they are?

Why do girls cry over the littlest thing?

Why do girls gossip, even about their friends?

Why do girls obsess about fashion?

Why do girls wear stupid little belts that don't even go through the belt loops?

Why do girls go to the bathroom in groups?

So you see, it's a two-way street. We don't understand them. They don't understand us.

Boys think they're the smartest and the best.

Madeleine, age 8

I hope this book will help change that.

It isn't going to be a guy-bashing book.

It isn't going to be a how-to-catch-a-guy book.

It isn't going to be a whine-and-complain book.

It's going to be a this-is-how-God-made-guys book and a this-is-why-guys-do-the-things-they-do book.

And in the end if you understand guys just a little bit better than you do now, then we'll have accomplished our goal. And you—and the guys you know—will be better off for it.

TO READ—

Genesis 1:26-31

TO THINK ABOUT—

1. Think of some examples of guy bashing you've seen in the media. Do you think guy bashing is considered more acceptable than girl bashing? Why, or why not?

2. What do you think are some of the biggest differences between guys and girls?

3. What do you think about nature versus nurture? In other words, are the differences between guys and girls designed by God, are they forced on us by the world, or both?

4. What one thing do you wish you understood about guys? What one thing do you wish guys understood about you?

Girls play with Barbies and boys play with boy stuff.
Bryssa, age 4

GIRLS TALK ABOUT GUYS

When do they stop being immature?

Why don't they let out their feelings?

Why do they always have to have the right answer?

Why are they are so gross?

What is so fascinating about hunting, fishing, etc.?

Why do they find disgusting things so funny?

Why do they burp all the time?

Why are they always asking, "What's wrong?"
like, 500 times in a row?

It's annoying when they leave really long messages on the
answering machine so your whole family can hear.

Why do they act macho all the time?

Why do they avoid conversation?

Why do they always feel the need to compete?

Why are they insensitive?

Why do they always have to win? EGOS!

Why do they always talk about girls' bodies?

They're obsessed with their cars, they lack fashion,
and they're moody.

They're so shy.

Why do they always change
around their friends?

It's so hard to read them.

They are so stubborn.

Why do guys always try to ignore problems?

What's with the tough act?

They only talk about cars, girls, and sports.

How can guys let things go so easily?

Why do they act like they just don't care?

Why do guys always want to be the boss?

Why don't guys listen to us when we talk?

Why don't they ever try to see our point of view?

Why can't they do two things at once?

It's annoying when you touch a guy's hair, and it's so
gelled up that it doesn't move, and they freak out.

Why can guys get over stuff so fast?

Why do they pretend everything's okay?

Guys have double standards for girls.

Why do they think degrading jokes are funny?

Guys are clueless about what
we're really trying to tell them.

Why do they hate talking on the phone?

Why do they say they'll call, then don't?

Why are they so possessive?

Why do they like sports so much?

Why do they care so much
about a girl's physical appearance?

It's annoying how when guys burp, it's cool,
but when a girl burps, it's gross.

Why don't they care about our feelings?

Why are they always trying to impress people?

Why won't they tell you what they're really thinking?

Why are they cocky, arrogant, and disrespectful?

How can a guy like you one day, then not like you the next?

Why do they always beat each other up,
then act like friends?

They are rude, they belch in public,
they hit each other, and they are immature.

They always show off.

Why are they always hitting someone?

Why are guys so fascinated
with getting dirty?

Who don't they ever ask for help or directions?

Why do they always start wrestling in places they shouldn't?

What's with all the disgusting body noises?

Guys always have a comment about everything.

Why don't any guys open doors for girls?

Why don't they look at you when they talk?

Why do they grunt?

They have such a small vocabulary.

I don't get how guys can daze out when watching TV.

Why are they so childish? Why do they act
like they're two years old?

Why don't they know how to do the dishes?

Why do they do dangerous things?

It's annoying that guys will talk to you when you're alone
but ignore you when their friends are around.

Why do they always have to win?

Chapter 2

Battle of the Sexes

In 1946 the musical *Annie Get Your Gun* opened on Broadway. It told the story of Annie Oakley, a backwoods, hillbilly sharpshooter who joined Buffalo Bill's Wild West Show. Things went great for Annie until her sharpshooting skills outshone those of Frank Butler, the star of the Wild West Show. Frank's ego took a terrible bruising, but that wasn't the worst of it. Annie soon found herself falling in love with Frank, worried that he couldn't, and wouldn't, love her back because of their sharpshooting competitiveness.

You'll have to rent the movie to see what happens.

Before Annie and Frank realize they're falling for one another, they sing a song that starts like this—

A: "I'm superior."

F: "You're inferior."

Girls like to play with cats.
Lauren, age 3

Both: Anything you can do I can do better; I can do anything better than you.

F: No, you can't.

A: Yes, I can.

F: No, you can't.

A: Yes, I can.

F: No, you can't.

A: Yes, I can, yes, I can!

F: I can shoot a partridge with a single cartridge.

A: I can get a sparrow with a bow and arrow.

F: I can do most anything.

A: Can you bake a pie?

F: No.

A: Neither can I.

And so on.

It's the age-old battle of the sexes, and it's been going on almost since the beginning of humanity.

When God first made man and woman, there was joy and happiness and true love between them. The man was thrilled that God made a woman to be his companion. When he first saw her, he said, "Finally! Bone of my bone, flesh of my flesh!" He knew that in the woman he had a partner and friend for life. In the Bible it says that man and woman were created to be the perfect complement to each other. (Check out Genesis 1:23-31.)

But all that changed when the serpent came on the scene. He convinced the woman to break the one and only rule God had made. The man and woman were surrounded

Boys like to hunt.
Tanner, age 7

by good things that God had given them to enjoy, but they were not allowed to eat any fruit from the tree of knowledge of good and evil. If they did, God said they would die.

Have you ever wondered why the serpent talked to the woman instead of the man? Is it because women enjoy conversation more? Is it because they're more gullible? Is it because they're more easily influenced? I don't know the answer, but the serpent made the right choice. He said to the woman, "Hey, all this talk about dying if you eat the fruit from that tree is nonsense. Trust me on this."

And she did.

And she ate.

And she convinced the man to eat too.

Have you ever wondered where the man was during all of this? Was he taking a nap? Was he watching a championship football game? Was he strolling through the garden? Some people think he was right there beside the woman the whole time the serpent was talking to her. If that's the case, why didn't he step up to the plate and protect her? Why didn't he chase the serpent away?

We'll never know.

But he didn't.

And worst of all, when the woman encouraged him to eat the forbidden fruit, he said, "Yeah, sure, why not? You're still alive, so it must be fine."

And that's when everything started going downhill.

The man and woman hadn't supported and taken care of each other the way they were supposed to. They hadn't looked out for each other's best interests. They hadn't honored each other as beloved creations of God.

Girls really like to play outside on the swingset.
Lauren, age 5

Most people know what happened next. God tracked them down and banished them from the garden where they'd been living. But something else happened. God said that not only was the relationship between him and the people broken, but the relationship between the two people themselves was broken as well. (Read Genesis 2:16-19.)

Suddenly, the relationship that was meant to be supportive and helpful and joyous and perfect was spoiled. And ever since then men and women have been struggling to get along with each other.

When you were a toddler, you probably didn't care at all whom you played with. Little boys and girls mix it up in church nurseries or in day care centers without any problem. They may not always play with the same toys, and they may not always like the same activities, but they seem to like each other well enough.

Then one day something horrible happens. You get a little older, a little wiser, and you discover cooties.

The boys think the girls have them.

The girls think the boys have them.

Cooties run rampant on every playground and in every classroom. Nothing is safe anymore. Life is forever changed. The world becomes a dangerous place. Aaaaugggh!

Do you remember the first time a boy came up to you and yelled, "You have cooties!" It can be devastating. Most little girls don't even know what cooties are, and then all of a sudden some nasty boy is announcing to the entire school that we have them. When I was in second grade, a boy told my best friend Mary that she had cooties. At first I thought she was going to cry. Then I thought maybe she

Girls like dolls.
Sage, age 6

was going to tell the principal or the lunch lady. But instead she did what any self-defensive little girl would do. She kicked the boy right in the shins. Really hard. It wasn't a very nice thing to do, but it seemed to make sense at the time.

The battle of the sexes is very real. Us versus them. Boys versus girls. Men versus women. Males versus females. Dogs versus cats. (When I was very young, I thought that the reason cats and dogs hated each other so much was because all the dogs were boys and all the cats were girls.)

Somehow we've gotten the idea that because men and women are different, they're in a competition to see who's better.

Since when does "different" mean "unequal"?

"Different" simply means "not the same." But it has nothing to do with the value or worth of the thing or the person.

In the case of gender, however, that's exactly what some people think.

For most of history the world was a very pro-male place. Men were considered better and more valuable than women. In fact, there are still countries where the birth of a baby girl is a sorrowful occasion, but the birth of a baby boy is cause for celebration.

Then, the Western world became a more female-friendly place. In fact, the way for a man to gain more value was to get in touch with his feminine side.

I think both of those ideas miss the point. The world should be pro-people. In other words, all of us should be

Girls like the wind (because I like the wind).
Eden, age 4

valued simply because we are human beings created by God. Because guys and girls tend to be different doesn't mean one or the other is better.

Many guys are better than girls at certain athletic skills. Guys tend to be stronger because they have more muscle mass. Does that make guys better than girls? No way.

Many girls are better than guys at understanding how someone is feeling. Girls tend to be more intuitive because of their brain structure. Does that make girls better than guys? No way.

Being better at something doesn't make people better, period. It just makes them different.

If you bake, you know that many recipes use exactly the same basic ingredients—flour, sugar, oil, eggs, baking soda, and salt. But each recipe uses those ingredients in different amounts. That's how people are. We are all made up of the same basic ingredients, but some of us have more of one ingredient and less of another. Does that make us better or worse? No. It just makes us different.

Every year the youth group that I help hosts a "Battle of the Sexes." Girls compete against guys in all kinds of activities, most of which are downright silly and meaningless. Over the past 10 years the guys and girls have won the contest an equal amount of times. When the guys win, it doesn't mean that they're better than the girls. It just means that, for that year they were more successful at stacking blocks, eating Cheez Whiz®, and doing dumb stuff with duct tape. When the girls win, it doesn't mean that they're better than the guys. It just means that, for that year they were more successful at burping out loud, playing

Girls like to jump rope.
Tanner, age 7

Twister®, and hopping up and down on one foot while blindfolded.

When it's designed to be fun, it's not bad for guys and girls to compete against each other. In fact, it can be a great way to build relationships between people who don't normally hang out in the same crowd.

However, there's a fine line between healthy competition and unhealthy derogation. It's one thing for the girls' team to laugh when the guys' faces get covered with whipped cream. It's another for the girls to say sneeringly, "Oh, man. What idiots! They are so stupid. Have you ever seen anyone act like such a slob?!"

When girls say stuff like that, what they really mean is, "Guys are so much stupider than girls. They're so much slobbier than girls. All in all, they're not as good as we are."

Guys and girls are both guilty of this kind of thing. Guys often make fun of girls for being airheads, ditzes, emotional basket cases, and irrational mood swingers. But since this book is for girls, we're going to focus on how girls act toward guys.

If you watch television at all, you know that guys are often portrayed as being childish, insensitive, sexist, dumb jocks. Women in the media are often shown rolling their eyes at men's behavior as if to say, "Honestly. Whose bright idea was it to create guys, anyway?!"

Well, it was God's idea. And since God's ideas are awesome, we'd better start looking at guys a little more closely and carefully. Part of the problem for teen girls is that all teen guys go through drastic changes during adolescence. You're seeing guys at what is probably their most unruly,

Boys like to go out and hunt.
Lauren, age 5

difficult, and hard-to-understand stage. The changes that take place between a guy's freshman year and senior year are huge. Sometimes it's hard to believe it's the same person that you knew three or four years earlier. Of course, the same is true of many girls. But on the whole guys go through more drastic maturity changes than girls do. We'll talk more about why that happens in a later chapter.

Helen Fisher is a world-renowned anthropologist. She once said something that makes a lot of sense. "I think men and women are like two feet. They need each other to get ahead."

In other words, if guys and girls, males and females, men and women, can somehow move beyond being annoyed with each other to being kind and understanding to each other, the whole world will be a better place. Girls, if you can start understanding the stage of life guys are going through, and if you can look at it with a patient and kind heart instead of an "oh, brother, here we go again" attitude, you'll be happier and so will the people around you.

Males and females not only compete over who's the best, but they also compete over who's got the toughest life. For a long time no, girls have gotten a lot of sympathy and attention from the world because of the disadvantages they've had. For instance, for a long time women couldn't vote. They couldn't own property. They couldn't make any financial decisions. They weren't welcome in many workplaces. They couldn't get the same education as men. They didn't have many of the basic rights and privileges that belong to all people.

But in America that's changed. Once they turn 18, girls can vote just like guys. They can own anything men can

Girls like Barbies and boys like cool stuff.
Austen, age 6

own. They can make their own financial decisions. They've entered every part of the workplace (of course, women still earn 80 cents on the dollar compared to men). They can get the same education. In fact, more women attend college now than men. All in all, men and women in America are closer to equal than they have ever been.

So is it still harder to be a girl? Most girls think so. Even a lot of guys think so. Girls deal with a lot of pressure to look a certain way. Body image is central to the female standard. A girl who doesn't fill all the perfect ideals of beauty can feel unworthy and valueless. On the other hand, guys seem to have more variety in what's acceptable as far as looks go. However, they're under intense pressure to be strong and well-built.

A few generations ago men naturally had bulked-up bodies because so many worked on farms or in other phys-ically demanding situations. Today, in order to have the right look, guys have to hit the weight room faithfully. While guys try to get bigger, girls try to get smaller. The pressure on both sexes is intense.

Another difficulty guys face is that, for some reason, it's okay for girls to have masculine traits but not for guys to have feminine traits. A girl who is strong and assertive doesn't get teased and mocked the same way a guy who is artistic and unathletic does. It's the same kind of double standard that we talked about with the BOYS ARE STUPID T-shirt. Being a boyish girl is acceptable. Being a girlish boy is not.

Perhaps the hardest thing about being a guy in today's world is the challenge of school. The academics aren't the problem. It's the school environment. Guys are wired to be competitive, to move around a lot, to be physical, to take

Boys like to dig holes.
Joshua, age 10

risks, and to push themselves to new limits. School has become a place where students are expected to sit still and to cooperate instead of compete. Teachers stand up front and do a lot of lecturing—another thing that can be difficult for guys. Males are more inclined to learn things by doing rather than by listening.

Think about it. Who usually gets reprimanded by teachers more often? Boys. They are constantly told to sit still, be quiet, pay attention, stop wiggling, stop poking other kids, stop this, stop that. In the comic strip *Calvin and Hobbes*, Calvin's worst nightmare is school. It's the place where he is never allowed to be himself. He spends most of his day daydreaming about dinosaurs, spaceships, dragons, and gory monsters . . . and then finds himself in the principal's office yet again, wondering what happened.

Girls, my challenge to you is to stop looking at guys as some weird subspecies that needs fixing. Stop looking at guys and wishing they were more like you. Stop looking at guys and saying to yourself, "Geez, I'm glad I'm not one of them." Stop assuming that guys have it easy and you have it hard.

Remember—when God made males and females, he said, "It is very good." He was talking about all people equally.

Guys and girls are different, there's no doubt. But "different" is not the same as "better." Maybe if we stop battling with the other sex, we'll finally be able to appreciate them more and will begin to see them as God sees them—loved, cherished, and awesome.

Boys like to play in the mud.
Matthew, age 7

"I think many young women have a vastly inaccurate picture of what is normal for them to think or to feel. They have been trained to accept that to be equal to men they must be the same in every respect, and they, and the men, are worse off for it."

—Wendy Shalit, *A Return to Modesty*

"Girls, it's in your best interest to let guys be males so they can reflect God's image the way he intended."

—Carrie Abbott of The Legacy Institute

I think boys are lucky because they get to go fishing more often than girls do.
Emily, age 9

TO READ—

Galatians 3:26-29

TO THINK ABOUT—

1. What is the hardest thing about being a teen girl? What do you think the hardest thing is about being a teen guy? (You might want to ask some guys what they think.)

2. What things do you think girls are better at than guys? What things do you think guys are better at than girls?

Girls say guys are better at—

being boys
getting along
football
strength
fixing electronics
forgiving people
staying calm
dealing with cars
most sports

Girls say girls are better at—

soccer
writing
helping other people
matching an outfit
school
dancing
singing

Boys like YuGiOh! cards.
Alyssa, age 7

reading
expressing themselves
getting a point across
accessorizing
listening
doing 10 things at one time

3. Do you think there's a lot of competition and comparison between guys and girls? If yes, think of some examples.

4. In your school are guys and girls treated differently? In what ways?

GIRLS THINK
THEY ARE BETTER AT . . .

talking
shopping
matching an outfit
writing
being helpful
soccer
caring
fashion
school
dancing
singing
reading
bathing
taking care of children
expressing feelings
opening up
communicating
telling true feelings
accessorizing
being sensitive
listening
thinking things through
artistic things
analyzing emotions
understanding
verbal things

matching their clothes
cooking
giving advice
striking up a conversation
etiquette
getting things done
working on a schedule
understanding how others feel
cheering people up
arguing
adapting to different situations
gracefulness
caring about what's happening around them
being smarter
acting their age
gossiping
persuasion
common sense
driving
being more sensible
using the toilet
gymnastics
swimming
controlling themselves
having a longer attention span
giving advice
losing
academics
compassion

Chapter 3

Boys Will Be Boys

Last summer I attended the wedding of two people
I'd known for almost eight years. The bride and groom,
who'd just graduated from college, had been high school
sweethearts. It was a hometown wedding, so there were
lots of close friends, lots of extended family, and lots of little kids in attendance.

About halfway through the reception I noticed that
many of the little girls had gathered in small groups. They
were giggling, making trips to the drinking fountain
together, skipping around the room, and enjoying each
other's company.

The little boys, on the other hand, had run out of good
public behavior resources. They'd already sat through a
wedding, waited in a long receiving line, and patiently
picked away at the vegetables on the reception dinner

Girls like to ride bikes on the street with helmets.
Lauren, age 3

plates. And they'd done it all in uncomfortable clothes. It was time for a break.

A few dads rounded up the boys and headed for the exit. I was curious, so I followed. I eventually found them all outside, gathered on the large lawn that surrounded the building. Some had taken off their shoes. All of them had untucked their shirts. A few had taken off their dress shirts to reveal their superhero-emblazoned T-shirts underneath. They all looked relieved to be outside, free from "sit still," "quit wiggling," "chew with your mouth closed," "don't burp in public," "stop sticking your tongue out at your brother," "quit playing with your food," and "for goodness sake, stop wiping your nose on your sleeve."

Do you know what all of those little boys were doing out there in the fresh air, far away from the restrictions and boredom of a wedding reception?

They were fighting.

In groups of two or three they were pummeling each other. These were four- and five-year-old boys, so it wasn't very strong pummeling, but it was pummeling nonetheless. And they seemed to be enjoying it immensely.

Now I have never understood the whole pummeling thing. Is it fun? Does it feel good? I don't know. But I do know this—given the choice, little boys would much rather pummel and push and knock each other down than go to a wedding.

There were no high school boys wrestling outside on the lawn that day. They stayed inside the reception hall, ate their meals, wondered if they were missing anything good on television, talked about their cars, and clanked their spoons wildly against the sides of their water glasses hoping to see the bride and groom make out in front of everyone. But if anyone had given them the option of going outside and wrestling instead of staying inside and behaving appropriately, I think at least some would have jumped at the chance to escape.

For the past 20 years I've been observing teenagers at school, at extracurricular activities, at home, at work, at church, and at play. In all that time I've noticed that there are some general differences that tend to show up between males and females. Now not all females fit the "girl" profile exactly, and not all males fit the "guy" profile perfectly. But in nine cases out of 10 guys and girls exhibit at least some of the characteristics that are commonly associated with their gender.

Here are my top 15 (I tried to stop at 10, but it wasn't possible) ways that teenage guys and girls are different. Before you read them, make your own list below. Then compare your list to mine when you finish the chapter.

TOP 10 (or 15) WAYS THAT TEEN GUYS AND GIRLS ARE DIFFERENT

1. _____

2. _____

3. _____

4. _____

Girls love to read.
Lauren, age 5

5. _____

6. _____

7. _____

8. _____

9. _____

10. _____

11. _____

12. _____

13. _____

14. _____

15. _____

TOP 15 WAYS
THAT TEEN GUYS AND GIRLS ARE DIFFERENT

(WARNING: Generalizations ahead—true for most people, most times)

1. Girls focus on people—guys focus on things.

Girls spend a lot of time and energy on their relationships. They talk on the phone. They e-mail. They write notes. It's important to girls to nurture and protect their friendships. In many ways their identity is wrapped up in who their friends are. The magazines they read have thousands of

Girl have really pretty dresses.
Sage, age 6

articles about how to be a good friend, how to tell if a friend is trustworthy, and how to talk to guys. Most girls' magazines are about relationships and fashion.

Guys spend a lot of time and energy on the things they own, whether it's cars, electronics, four-wheelers, or electric guitars. It's important to guys to know how their stuff works. They can happily spend hours messing with their guitar amp wiring or their dirt bike engine. The magazines they read have thousands of articles about how to win a certain PlayStation® game, how to work on an exhaust system, and how to reprogram computers. Most guys' magazines are about things and activities.

2. Girls giggle—boys wiggle.

The freshman choir in my town's high school has 75 students in it. About two thirds are girls, and the rest are guys. During rehearsal, when the teacher stops in the middle of a song in order to give a direction to the class, the same thing always happens—the girls start whispering and giggling, and the guys start poking each other and wiggling around. I've watched it happen hundreds of times, and it's always the same. As soon as there's a break in the teaching action, the girls talk, the boys get physical. I've seen a guy reach back three rows, whack someone upside the head, and get back to his own seat in mere seconds. And I've listened to a girl give an overview of what happened to all of her friends over the past weekend, what happened during the first three hours of that day, and what she's planning on wearing tomorrow all in a matter of seconds. Given an opportunity, girls will talk, and boys will punch or poke somebody.

Boys like transportation things like motorbikes, planes, and racecars.
Madeleine, age 8

3. Girls cooperate—guys compete.

It's important to girls to keep everyone happy, so when a disagreement or conflict arises, they try to work it out. They might compromise. They might change the rules to keep everyone happy. They might take a break and analyze everyone's feelings. But they will make every effort to work together so everyone stays friends. A girl's prestige is wrapped up in her relationships, so she'll do whatever she can to protect them.

It's important to guys to win. When a disagreement or conflict arises, they won't bend the rules or change the strategy just to keep someone happy. They'll just try harder. Playing by the rules is very important to them. It gives them a sense of security. A guy's prestige is wrapped up in his accomplishments and abilities, so he'll do whatever he can to be the top dog.

4. Girls are cautious and controlled—guys are impulsive and risky.

Girls usually live within the conventional rules. They stop and think about the consequences of their actions beforehand. They get fewer speeding tickets than guys, make fewer trips to the emergency room, and get in trouble with authorities less often. Girls tend to be more careful, are more aware of the risks inherent in dangerous situations, and are more likely to say, "It's just not worth the risk."

Guys like to push the envelope. They move fast, test the limits, and stretch the boundaries. They get a thrill out of speed, and they're usually very willing to try new things. They tend to count the costs and risks after instead of before. They get in trouble more often in school, at home,

Girls scream when boys chase them.
Tanner, age 7

and in the community for engaging in dangerous, silly, and sometimes illegal behavior.

5. Girls stab in the back—guys punch in the face.

Girls are interested in talking. Girls are interested in people. Girls are interested in talking about people. Gossip is truly a feminine art. Girls are masters at tearing each other down through words that may sound sweet but are really sour. "So . . . what did you think of Christine's outfit today?" really means, "Did you see those pants she was wearing? They made her look huge! And that shirt was disgusting. Who does she think she is?!" When a girl has a score to settle with another girl, she usually does it with words, and often those words are spoken indirectly, behind the other person's back, rather than honestly, face to face.

When a guy has a bone to pick with another guy, he usually does it face to face, with actions instead of words. Guys tend to face their problems head-on, deal with them, and then let go of them. They'd rather hit someone in the face than talk about him behind his back.

6. Girls make conversation—guys make noise.

Girls love to talk. Girls love people. Girls love to talk with people. Girls use the telephone as a bonding tool. A girl can spend hours talking to her friend on the phone about everything from fashion to who has a crush on whom to what Mrs. Jackson said in American lit to her weekend plans to her new favorite outfit to blah, blah, blah, blah. Girls talk every chance they get—between classes, in chat rooms, during class, while shopping, and while doing homework.

Boys like to play war.
Lauren, age 5

Guys love to make noise. They cheer. They grunt. They mimic engines. They roar. They do the *Home Improvement* wolf bark. They are masters at using sounds to make a point or embellish a story or add excitement to an activity. Some of their better known noises are "yo" and "'sup?"

7. Girls shop—guys buy stuff.

Mall endurance is definitely a female gift. Hour after hour, store after store, rack after rack, and item after item, shopping doesn't fatigue a female. It energizes her. It's fun. It's entertaining. It's a way to bond with friends.

Guys don't shop. They buy stuff. If they need jeans, they go to the store, find a pair they like, and buy them. The concept of looking at 14 different stores, trying on each pair to check for fit, and comparing styles sends a guy into a tailspin. It makes him nauseated. It makes him shake his head back and forth in disgust and say, "Girls. What's with them, anyway?"

8. Girls wear outfits—guys wear clothes.

Girls are fashion experts. They have access to countless magazines and catalogs that provide fashion tips and secrets. They have a gazillion more fashion choices than guys do. They are accessory studettes. They know how to mix, match, and rearrange things a thousand different ways. Of course, this means they sometimes need several hours to get ready in the morning.

Guys wear clothes, mostly because they're required. Since nudity is not an option in public, guys are forced to throw something on each morning. Sometimes it matches, sometimes it doesn't. Sometimes it's clean, sometimes it's not. Sometimes it's coordinated, sometimes it's not. Though their clothes aren't usually a source of great concern, guys' hair is another matter. They've been known to use an entire bottle of gel trying to get their bangs and sideburns to lie just right.

9. Girls analyze everything—guys deal with stuff.

When something unexpected or painful happens to a girl, she takes the situation, breaks it into a million little pieces, examines each one in detail, turns it around and around in her head trying to figure out what happened, puts the pieces back together, and then repeats the process over and over and over. "Did I do something wrong? Is it something I said? Is she mad at me? Did I make a mistake? Why does he hate me? Why did she say that to me? Should I transfer to a different school? Should I call and apologize? Should I just pretend that nothing happened? How will I ever face everyone at school tomorrow?" And so on.

When something unexpected or painful happens to a guy, he moves into the private, quiet spot in his brain, checks it out, decides on a response or solution, deals with it, and then moves on with his life. How do they do it?!

10. Girls use their intuition—guys use information.

Girls often rely on their intuition to make decisions or to assess a situation. Things might feel wrong. Someone might make a bad impression. She might have a strange sense of something being not quite right. She can tell who likes whom just by observing the way they act. It's an amazing thing, but a girl's intuition is very real. And most of the time it's very accurate.

Guys usually focus on information. If a guy sees someone crying, he'll know that person is upset. But if the upset person is trying to hide their feelings or isn't totally open about what the problem is, a guy will assume everything is all right. Guys don't usually understand the subtle nuances of a person's behavior.

11. Girls focus on intimacy—guys focus on independence.

A girl's best friend is the most important person in her life. They talk about everything. They share every thought, every emotion, and every personal detail about life. They strive to know each other better and better as time goes on. Their closeness is a measure of their worth, and they take their friendship to new levels at every possible chance.

A guy's group of friends is important to him. But equally important is his status as an independent individual. Guys tend to break away from their parents earlier than girls do. They want to make their own decisions, take care of themselves, and be their own men as soon as possible. Though friends are important, developing themselves as independent individuals is equally if not more important.

12. Girls like chick flicks—guys like action films.

Girls are all about relationships, so naturally they enjoy movies that tell a story about the connections between people. They especially enjoy falling-in-love stories, and because of their ability to put themselves into another person's shoes, they can really feel the emotions of the actors. In fact, girls have been known to watch a particularly romantic scene, rewind the video, watch the scene again, rewind the video, watch the scene again . . . girls can enter into the story that's playing on the screen or television and make it their own.

Boys like to swim.
Matthew, age 7

Guys, on the other hand, like movies with action, suspense, horror, and silly jokes. Slow-moving stories don't keep a guy's attention, and guys have been known to fall asleep during chick flicks. In the movie *How to Lose a Guy in 10 Days*, there's a scene where Andie (Kate Hudson) and Ben (Matthew McConaughey) are watching *Sleepless in Seattle* at a theater. It's their first movie date, and in order to impress Andie Ben is pretending that he absolutely loves the movie when, in fact, he'd rather be at home watching basketball or playing poker with his buddies. But he doesn't tell Andie that . . . not yet, anyway.

13. Girls cry—guys hide it.

Girls can be like leaky faucets. Some have an everlasting supply of tears. I cry when I see Kodak commercials, during the Olympic opening ceremonies, and watching 4th of July fireworks (and a lot of other times as well). My cousin cries every time she's in an airport. "I can't help it," she told me. "I watch all those people saying goodbye to each other before they get on their planes, and my heart just breaks for them!" Girls have been known to cry when they're sad, when they're happy, when they're lonely, when they're angry, when they're frustrated, when they're tired, when they watch a sad movie, when they read a sad book, and when their pet gerbil dies.

Guys cry. But it doesn't often happen in public. And it isn't usually accompanied by ranting and raving. It's more often a private affair, just the guy by himself or the guy with one close friend. And it's usually in response to a very specific event or situation that's been building up inside for a while. Guys are incredulous at girls who cry at something that's happening on the television screen. In such instances

When boys are sad or lonely they might cry.
Emily, age 9

they've been known to say such things as, "Don't tell me you're crying again!?" or "Are you actually crying because that kid's dog died?! It's just a stupid movie!"

14. Girls go to the bathroom in groups—guys go to the bathroom solo.

This one really doesn't need much explanation. The plain and simple fact is that girls travel en masse (that means all together in a big group) when heading to the bathroom. Guys do not understand this. It's a big, fat, giant mystery to them. In fact, many girls don't understand it either. For girls the bathroom is a meeting place. It's a place to talk about the day, to visit, to bond, to solve problems, to have a good cry, and so much more. If a girl went to the bathroom alone, she'd have wasted five minutes of her life that she could have spent with a friend. What a waste of time!

Guys go to the bathroom alone. They don't want to "share their feelings," "get in touch with their emotions," or "talk about the day." They just want to go to the bathroom and get on with their lives. The bathroom is merely a utilitarian place for guys. It holds no social value. It's a necessary place that should be used for one thing and one thing only. Guys, however, do sometimes huddle and gather in the locker room, but that's another topic for another time.

15. Girls get ready for school—guys get dressed.

If a girl needs to leave for school at 8 a.m., she will probably get up by at least 7 a.m. Some girls might get up as early as 6 a.m. That allows time to shower, fix hair, put on makeup, try on several different outfits, accessorize, brush teeth, and maybe grab a quick breakfast.

Boys get in trouble more.
Alyssa, age 7

If a guy needs to leave for school at 8 a.m., he will probably get up at about 7:45. Some might get up as early as 7:40. That allows time to shower, shake out hair, throw on some clothes, brush teeth, and grab a hearty breakfast.

Don't ask me how this works, but it does.

BONUS (I tried to stop at 15 . . . really, I did.)

Girls view shoes as a fashion statement—guys view shoes as foot coverings.

When I go on trips with high school students, the girls almost always pack enough shoes to wear a different pair each day. They can choose between casual sandals, fancy sandals, comfortable Doc Martens, pointy-toed boots, flip-flops, slip-ons, cute tennies, fancy strappy things, and maybe something comfortable to walk in.

Guys pack gym shoes.

There you have it. The top 15 ways, plus a bonus, that teen guys and girls are different. The differences are very real. We've all seen them with our own eyes. The question we have to ask now is why are the differences there in the first place?

Boys like to play basketball and soccer.
Bryssa, age 4

TO READ—

Genesis 4:1-9

TO THINK ABOUT—

1. Which of the female stereotypes above fit you? Which ones don't?

2. Do girls and guys feel pressured to fit a certain mold? In other words, are girls and guys expected to act certain ways?

3. Which of the differences talked about above are the hardest for you personally to understand and deal with?

4. If the story you just read about Cain and Abel was about two sisters, how would it have been different?

 Girls like to play with nice worms, caterpillars, and water bugs.
Lauren, age 3

GIRLS THINK
GUYS ARE BETTER AT . . .

burping
wrestling
football
baseball
being boys
getting along
blowing off unimportant things
video games
math
science
fixing things
electronics
forgiving
staying calm
cars
mechanical things
dealing with cars
acting macho
letting things not bother them
racing
not holding a grudge
hiding emotions
taking it easy
working hard
keeping fit

being relaxed
playing guitar
rock climbing
lifting weights
shooting guns
keeping a secret
getting over hurt feelings
controlling emotions
not worrying about appearance
eating gross food
public speaking
acting dumb
not being judgmental
lifting heavy things
being insensitive
going to the bathroom standing up
showing off
not paying attention
sitting on the couch
bragging
building things
making quick decisions
eating
playing with fire
running
throwing

Chapter 4

Brain Matters

(Warning label: This chapter contains data that is true for nine out of 10 people. Maybe you are that other one in 10 but read on anyway. Also, there are no health risks associated with reading this information . . .)

Brain Quiz

How much do you know about the human brain?
Check your brain's brains with this quiz.

1) **The brain is divided into how many halves? (Hint: halves . . .)**
   a) one
   b) two
   c) three
   d) 7.2

Boys run from attacking girls.
Tanner, age 7

2)The halves of the brain are called
   a) countries
   b) departments
   c) continents
   d) hemispheres

3) The gross and icky outer layer of the brain that looks like a plate of gigantic gray spaghetti noodles is called
   a) the gross and icky outer layer of the brain
   b) cerebrum
   c) noodlistonorium
   d) Frankensteinopticrusis

4) Which of these lists is in correct order of brain size from smallest to largest?
   a) mouse, man, woman
   b) man, mouse, woman
   c) woman, mouse, man
   d) mouse, woman, man

5) The bridge that connects the two halves of the brain (big hint for question 1) is called the
   a) Golden Gate Bridge
   b) corpus callosum
   c) London Bridge
   d) Corpus Christi

6) The best way to prevent brain injury while riding a bike is to
   a) wear a bandana
   b) wear a medically approved biking helmet
   c) wear a baseball cap
   d) wear your hair in braids

Girls like to write stories.
Lauren, age 5

7) IQ, which is designed to measure a person's educational potential, is short for
   a) Interesting Quotes
   b) Itty-bitty Quacks
   c) Illinois Quarters
   d) Intelligence Quotient

8) If you needed a rhyming word for "brain," a good choice would be
   a) ocean
   b) toenail polish
   c) biology
   d) train

9) When eating a bowl of ice cream on a hot day, some people experience
   a) brain meltdown
   b) brain warts
   c) brain attack
   d) brain freeze

10) The brain is located in what part of the human body?
   a) the elbow
   b) the big toe
   c) the head
   d) the left earlobe

11) A really smart student is sometimes called
   a) a smart foot
   b) a beatnik
   c) a brainiac
   d) Lester

Correct Answers
1)b, 2)d, 3)b, 4)d, 5)b, 6)b, 7)d, 8)d, 9)d, 10)c, 11)c

Girls like to do art.
Sage, age 6

In case you hadn't realized, 1990 through 1999 was the Decade of the Brain. No kidding. It was made official by Presidential Proclamation #6158.

"Now therefore, I, George Bush, President of the United States of America, do hereby proclaim the decade beginning January 1, 1990, as the Decade of the Brain. I call upon all public officials and the people of the United States to observe that decade with appropriate programs, ceremonies, and activities."

I don't know about you, but I sure didn't "observe the decade with appropriate programs, ceremonies, and activities." I didn't have any brain parties during the '90s. I didn't attend any brain parades, any brain celebrations, or any brain dances. I didn't watch any brain movies, read any brain magazines, or buy any brain posters. In fact, at the time I didn't even know that the '90s was the Decade of the Brain. (I'll be honest—even if I had known, I probably wouldn't have hung a poster of a disgusting glob of quivering gray mush on the back of my bedroom door.)

The Decade of the Brain pretty much passed me by. How about you?

Since that time, however, I've learned quite a bit about the human brain. In fact, I've done all the things that I should have done but didn't during the Decade of the Brain. I've read brain books and brain magazines—you wouldn't believe how many there are. I've watched brain movies. I've studied the brain—not a real one, of course. I've talked to hundreds of people about the brain. Through all of that I've learned that the brain—even though it is pretty gross to look at—is one of the most fascinating, amazing, and awesome things that God created. Scientists

Girls like butterflies.
Eden, age 4

seem to agree because they are striving to learn more and more about how it works every day.

One thing they've learned is that the male brain and the female brain are—surprise, surprise!—different in many ways. If the scientists had just spent a few days hanging out in a junior or senior high school, they probably could have figured this out a long, long time ago, don't you think? In any case the scientific community can now say without any hesitation—hey, guys! hey, girls! your brains are different and unique, not just as individuals, but also as a complete gender group.

In fact, if scientists were to look at actual brains—and thank goodness that most of us don't have to look at real brains because honestly, that would pretty much ruin our appetites, don't you think?—they would be able to correctly identify them as either male or female 19 times out of 20. In other words, almost all male brains have certain unique characteristics, and almost all female brains have certain unique characteristics.

Cartoonists have a great time poking fun at male and female brains. Here's one cartoonist's "scientific" diagram of a male teen brain:

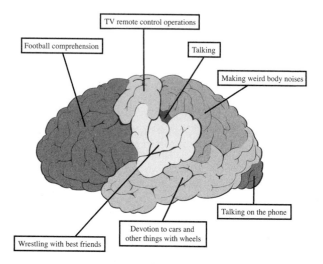

And here's a cartoonist's diagram of what a female teen brain might look like:

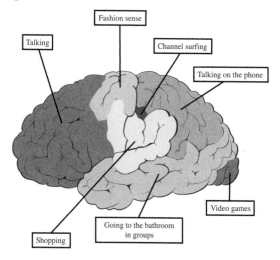

Obviously, real brain differences aren't like the ones in the diagrams. A lot of what we're going to talk about in the next few chapters is based on the information in this chapter. The brain is sort of like a computer operating system. It affects every action, decision, behavior, and characteristic of a person. Understanding how the brain works can help you understand people. So understanding how the male brain works will help you understand guys. There will still be a lot of mysteries about why some boys say what they say, do what they do, and act the way they act, but the mysteries won't be quite so, um, mysterious.

So even if you hate science, biology and anatomy, don't skip the rest of this chapter. I guarantee that it will help you figure out what's going on in the world of guys.

Hemispheres and bridges—the side-to-side stuff

Every human brain is divided into two halves that are called the right hemisphere and the left hemisphere. The two halves are connected by a bundle of nerves that is called the corpus callosum. Since this isn't a science book, let's call these things the right side, the left side, and the bridge.

Each side of the brain has a specialty. The right side specializes in spatial things, such as being able to track an object as it moves through the air, being able to imagine what a two-dimensional drawing would look like as a three-dimensional object, or being able to calculate how fast something needs to move in order to get from point A to point B in a certain amount of time. These are just a few examples.

Boys stand up, and girls sit down
(boys sit if they have to go poop).
Austen, age 6

The left side specializes in language. That would be anything that has to do with talking, organizing thoughts, understanding verbal instructions, or reading and writing, to name a few.

When babies are first conceived, their brains are exactly the same. In fact, up until the time fetuses are six weeks old, they all have female brains. Yes, even the boys. At six weeks something amazing happens. Chemicals and hormones start rinsing over the male brain, in effect giving it a brainwash, and from that point on it begins to develop differently from a female brain. When babies are born, their brains are already distinctly male or female in several different ways.

First, males have stronger right brains than left brains while females have stronger left brains than right brains. This means guys are better at looking at a Lego diagram and then building it, and girls are better at reading. Guys are better at parallel parking, and girls are better at understanding lectures. Guys are better at calculating how hard and fast to throw a baseball from left field so that it arrives exactly at first base, and girls are better at answering essay questions.

Not only are the two sides of the brains different in guys and girls, but the bridge is also different too. In girls' brains its much bigger and stronger. What does that mean? It means that girls are able to use their bridge to dance back and forth between the two sides of their brains at a dizzying speed. In fact, girls don't even have to dance back and forth. They can actually plant one foot (not an actual foot, of course, but you get the idea) on each side of the brain and live in both the left and right brain worlds at the same time.

Boys like fishing.
Joshua, age 10

If you understand what this means, you will take a huge step toward understanding one of the biggest differences between you and guys.

Basically, girls are able to multitask easily while guys are more likely to do one task at a time. Girls can paint their toenails, talk on the phone, finish up their homework, type an e-mail, and plan what they're going to wear the next day . . . all at the same time! Well, maybe not all of those things, but think about it. It's not a problem for most girls to do two things at once. You're able to use both sides of your brain to juggle different activities and thoughts without much problem.

Guys, on the other hand, are biologically unable to do this. Have you ever noticed what happens when you try to talk to your dad or brother or guy friend while he's watching TV? Either he ignores you (at least it seems like he's ignoring you), or else he blows up and says, "Can't you see I'm watching TV?" In fact, he's not ignoring you. His brain is busy focusing on something else. When you try to talk to him, it's almost as though you're asking him to shut down one part of his brain, pick himself up, take a long walk over his brain bridge (which isn't as big as yours, remember), get to the other part of his brain, turn it on, and then pay attention to you. You're asking him to do the impossible. And when you finally nag him so long that he responds, he might yell because you've really "messed with his mind," so to speak.

It would be better for you to give a little bit of warning, like saying, "When you're finished, could I talk to you?" or, "I need to ask you something during a commercial, Dad." This is true whether the guy is watching TV, reading the

Boys like to destroy things.
Madeleine, age 8

paper, working on his car, building something, or anything else that requires his concentration.

On the other hand you need to understand that when a brother, dad, or other guy tries to talk to you, he might feel like he's being ignored if you don't stop what you're doing and pay attention to him. Sure, you can finish reading your magazine and reorganizing your closet while he talks, but since he can't do all those things at once, it might seem to him like you're tuning him out.

A man named Bill Farrel wrote a book called *Men Are Like Waffles, Women Are Like Spaghetti*. You know how waffles have all those little squares in them? Farrel says that a guy's brain makes him approach life as if it's a waffle with lots of tiny squares or boxes. He opens one box, checks it out, takes care of it, closes it up, then goes on to the next box, opens it, checks it out, takes care of it, and so on. Girls, on the other hand, approach life like spaghetti. There can be a million noodles on a plate of spaghetti, but you can't tell where one starts and the other ends. They all run together, intersecting, going everywhere at the same time.

All of this stuff about left and right brains and big bridges and little bridges is true for most people, but there are always exceptions. There are some guys who are great at multitasking. There are some women who are awesome mechanical engineers. That doesn't make any of them less male or less female. It just makes them great multitaskers and great engineers.

"One thing girls like to do is be in clubs. I'm in a club with my sister and her friend. We're trying to raise money so we can buy stuff."
Linni, 6

Layers and sections—the up and down stuff

Not only do brains have different sides, but they also have different layers and sections. Without getting into all the science babble and without trying to explain everything, here are the basic differences between guys and girls and their up-and-down brain abilities.

First, when an experience creates some kind of emotion in guys or girls, their brains will deal with it differently. Let's say the emotion enters the brain in the middle layer. In a girl that emotion will then move up one layer to the thinking and analyzing part of the brain. Think of a time when you've been upset or sad. How did you respond? Usually, girls will start analyzing the emotion. What happened? Why do I feel like this? What did I do wrong? Why is my mom so mad at me? How am I ever going to face my friends tomorrow?

After analyzing, girls move onto the next phase, something guys call "overanalyzing." You know what I'm talking about. Some girls get so obsessed with thinking about things that they nearly drive themselves nuts. They can't get over it. They can't forget it. They can't drop it and move on with life. No, first they must break the problem down into miniscule, teensy-weensy pieces and analyze, then overanalyze, each one of them. They might discuss each teensy-weensy piece with their friends. They might journal about it. They might write a poem about it. Then when they put the teensy weensy pieces back together, they break the whole thing up again into different teensy weensy pieces. And on it goes.

When boys win a game they show off
because they think they are so cool.
Emily, age 9

When a guy has an emotional experience, it tends to move down from the middle layer to the lower layer. This is a very basic part of the brain, sometimes referred to as the "fight or flight" center. Guys usually respond to emotional experiences in one of two ways. Either they fight it head on, or they run from it.

Guys "fight" in response to an emotion in different ways. If they're angry, they might punch a wall or slam a door. They might yell at someone. They might play their drums really loudly. The might go out and round up some friends to play a really hard-hitting game of football.

If they don't fight, guys might flee. At least that's what it looks like to other people. Guys are often accused of running away from, ignoring, or suppressing their emotions. In fact, more likely the guy is just setting the emotion aside—for a while—while he thinks about it and tries to figure out what to do. For guys, emotions are problems to be solved. If a guy feels angry, he wants to fix it. If he feels sad, he wants to fix it. He doesn't enjoy analyzing it and working through it like girls do. And he certainly doesn't want to drag it out any longer than necessary. He wants to deal with it and be done with it.

A guy can flee in different ways. He might shut himself in his room and spend some time alone thinking about things. I know one guy who writes songs when he's feeling upset or sad. That's his "solution" to the "problem." Some guys might act like nothing's wrong until they've had some time to think things through. Some guys might call a friend to talk about the situation, but this doesn't happen very often. Guys are more independent than girls, and they prefer to solve these things alone rather than with a group of people.

Boys are handsome.
Alyssa, age 7

We'll talk more about guys and emotions later on. For now it's enough for you to know that the brain of a guy and the brain of a girl handle emotions differently. But then, you probably already guessed that, right?

There's another brain difference between guys and girls that you've probably noticed. When outside information enters the brain, it takes a certain amount of "brain stimulation" to get the person's attention. A guy's brain requires more "brain stimulation" in order to keep from getting bored. In other words, if a class of elementary-aged kids were told to sit at their desks and color a picture, the boys would probably get bored faster. Coloring a picture might not provide enough stimulation to keep a boy's attention for more than, oh, a few minutes. But a girl might be able to stick to the task much longer. A little boy needs a lot of excitement and energy to stay interested in something. To some degree that's true of guys for their entire lives. It probably wouldn't surprise you to learn that more boys than girls hate school. It's not because they don't want to learn. It's because school, for boys, is quite often biologically boring to their brains.

Besides brain differences there are also hormonal differences between guys and girls that have a huge effect on behavior and body development. The hormone we'll talk about the most is testosterone. Some people refer to it as the "He Hormone." Both guys and girls have testosterone, but guys have 10 to 20 times more than girls do. And during puberty, a guy's brain and body are being flooded with testosterone. That's what causes their voices to drop, body and facial hair to grow, muscles to start developing, and sex drive to kick in. Testosterone is also thought to be what

Boys like to go outside.
Bryssa, age 4

makes guys more physically active, more willing to take risks, and more competitive.

Brains and testosterone: They don't cause all the differences between you and guys, but they sure are responsible for a lot of them. In the next few chapters let's look at the top five "guy things" that girls don't understand about guys and see if we can start to make some sense of them.

TO READ—

Psalm 139:13-16

TO THINK ABOUT—

1. In what ways do you fit the typical female brain profile—multitasking, strong language skills, emotional analysis? In what ways don't you fit the typical female brain profile?

2. Think of some guys you know. How do they/don't they fit the typical male brain profile?

3. Why do you think God designed males and females so differently?

4. How will it make a difference in your day-to-day life if you understand how guys' and girls' brains are different?

Girls like sparkly jewelry but boys don't.
Lauren, age 3

GUYS TALK ABOUT GIRLS

How they don't think logically

Incessant talking

Gossip

Emotions

They're always saying "ohhh" and "ahhh, that's so cute"

They take so long to get ready, even if they are just going to Subway

Cliques

They comb their hair every five seconds

When they "can't find anything to wear"

They get mad at you for nothing

When they talk in whispers

When they think they need makeup to be pretty

How intensely insulted they can make someone feel

Chapter 5

Bravado, Brawn, and Bullies— Guys and Toughness

> **bravado** *n* arrogant defiance or menace, affectation of reckless bravery
>
> **brawn** *n* flesh, firm muscle, strength
>
> **bullies** *n pl* quarrelsome, swaggering, blustery fellows

"Chicks dig scars."

—John, 17

"I wish girls understood that guys have to play paintball. I can't live without it."

—Joey, 13

"Why do guys always try to act all macho when they aren't?"

—Shannon, 16

Every summer Mark and I take teenagers from our town to a camp in North Carolina where we join hundreds of other teens from all over the United States for an awesome week of fun, laughter, thrills, and "meeting interesting people from other places," which really means "scoping out the crowd to see if there's anyone cute I might want to meet."

"Some boys think they are sooooooooo cool."

—Hannah, 8

During last summer's trip I was sitting in the snack shop one afternoon when three senior guys from my town—Kurt, Shane, and Justin—walked in, laughing and pushing each other around. When they sat down I said, "What have you guys been doing all afternoon?" In unison they lifted their shirts and showed me their stomachs and chests, all of which were covered with nasty-looking, round, bright red welts. The mother in me kicked into high gear, and I said worriedly, "What happened to you? Are you okay? Do we need to go to the infirmary?"

They all three grinned broadly and said, "We've been playing Ping-Pong Pelt."

"Ping-Pong Pelt?" I asked. "Never heard of it."

"It's so cool," said one. "You play Ping-Pong to five points. Whoever loses has to lift up his shirt. The other guy gets to hit the Ping-Pong ball as hard as he can at the loser. And this," he pointed to one of his more deadly looking welts, "is what happens."

They all nodded and laughed and started showing me their many battle scars.

Girls love to be kind to other people.
Lauren, age 5

"And you actually want to play this game?" I asked.

"Oh, man. It's so great," said Kurt. "I mean, yeah, it hurts like anything, especially when Alex wins," he referred to one of the tallest, strongest, toughest guys in our group, "but it is so awesome to stand there and take it like a man." I couldn't be sure, but it looked like Kurt's chest was puffing out with the merest hint of studly pride.

"It's awesome?" I said incredulously.

"Yeah, totally, it's so great," they all said.

"So let me get this straight. You play to five; the loser lifts up his shirt, the winner whacks the Ping-Pong ball at the loser, it hurts like the dickens, you get an ugly, nasty, disgusting welt, and then you play all over again. Is that right?" I asked.

"Yeah, yeah, that's it exactly," they said.

"And the point is?" I asked.

"Like I said," answered Kurt, "to show you can take it. Plus the girls think it's really cool when we show them our welts."

> The hardest thing about being a guy is thinking you have to live up to some macho image. It takes a lot to let go of your ego and rely on God.
>
> —Rob, 18

Yeah, right, I thought to myself. There's nothing like a guy with a stomach and chest full of welts to catch a girl's eye.

From the time they're very young boys are all about competition, acting tough, being number one, and challenging

Girls like pink.
Sage, age 6

anyone who stands in their way. Think about the costumes little boys wear—capes, masks, swords, and underpants on the outside of their sweatpants to emulate the look of a superhero leotard. And then there are the guns. Everything is a gun. Sticks are guns. Their sister's Barbie dolls are guns. Pencils are guns. Even bread is a gun when it's bitten the right way.

Where does this behavior come from? Are boys taught to be tough and rough, macho and muscular, cool and competitive? Or is it possible that they are wired in such a way that those things come naturally?

"The hardest thing about being a guy is living up to everyone's expectations to be tough and strong."

—Joe, 19

John Eldrege, an author, says that every male is part warrior. Every man, guy, and little boy desperately wants a battle to fight. After raising three sons and getting to know hundreds of young men, I agree with him. There's something about battling an enemy that comes naturally to most guys.

Competition and athletics

There are some very specific biological reasons that guys tend to be competitive, physically active, macho, tough, and all those other typical "guy things." First, guys have a much higher level of the hormone testosterone than girls do. During the teen years the level is even higher as guys go through puberty and adolescence. In many ways testosterone makes guys the way they are. As we talked about in an earlier chapter, testosterone is what causes a guy's voice to lower, facial hair to grow, and muscles to develop. It also affects attitude and behavior.

"The hardest thing about being a guy is trying to keep your own identity."

—Ben, 17

Second, guys are very focused on doing. They do, do, do, all with the goal of succeeding. A guy's image is often based on how well he does things. He defines his worth based on his accomplishments and successes, whereas girls often base their worth on the quality of their friendships.

For that reason guys are often competing with each other to see who's "top dog." Groups of guy friends are based on hierarchy. That is, they know who's "in charge" and who calls the shots. They're all considered important, but some are definitely leaders, some are supporters, and some are followers. Girls, on the other hand, tend to be egalitarian, which means they all hold positions of equal control and value. Girls cooperate as a way to stay close. Guys compete as a way to stay close.

That might sound weird, but think about it for a minute. Haven't you seen guys who are really good friends giving each other a hard time? In a guy's world that's a sign of honor and respect. It's almost like saying, "I value you enough to compete with you. You're my friend, and so I know we can challenge each other safely." Guys see competition as acceptable and enjoyable, but girls see it as a threat to intimacy.

This is one of the main reasons many guys love athletics—it provides an opportunity for socially acceptable

Boys like to write stories.
Lauren, age 5

competition. On the playing field guys are allowed to "battle" each other, to knock their "enemies" down, and to pursue victory at all costs. They also get to take advantage of their strong spatial skills as they calculate how fast to run, how hard to throw, and how far to shoot. In sports guys get to utilize their strengths, which gives them a feeling of success.

It's not just the physical and spatial aspect of sports that draws guys. There's also an emotional aspect. Yes, that's right—emotional. Right before a big race or game a guy's testosterone level rises by almost 40 percent, which gives him the added "oomph" he needs to pursue victory. If he wins the game or race, his testosterone rises even more, giving him a surge of dopamine, a brain chemical that provides a sense of euphoria or the "winner's rush." This emotional response can become almost addicting for some people. Just for the record, testosterone also plays a role in girls' athletic events, but the levels don't rise nearly as much as in guys.

The hardest thing about a teen guy is having to be "cool."

—Trevor, 12

What about those guys who don't engage in sports but can watch them on television all day? What keeps them glued to the screen for hours on end? Guys can actually experience the same kind of "winner's high" simply by watching sports. If a guy's favorite team wins a game, whether he's watching it live in person or live on television, his testosterone level will rise, he'll experience a rush of dopamine, and he'll experience the same euphoria as the athletes do. That might be why professional athletes are the

Girls talk about girl stuff, and boys talk about airplanes and rescue heroes and baseball and cool stuff.

Austen, age 6

highest paid people in the world. They don't just provide entertainment. They actually provide a biological effect that keeps people coming back for more.

> "The hardest thing about being a teen guy is the pressure to do risky things without wimping out."
>
> —Mark, 15

As long as we're talking about sports on television, let's talk about another television issue, namely—why do guys channel surf like madmen?

If you've ever watched TV with your brother, dad, or a guy, you know that unless he's totally mesmerized by a show, his favorite hobby is to hold the remote control straight out toward the television. His thumb is in the bent, ready-to-click position. His eyes are focused blindly at the channel menu in the screen's corner. His brain is set to "megasurf." And in the blink of an eye he clicks through all 280 stations . . . twice.

Remember that in the brain chapter I told you a guy's brain requires a higher level of stimulation to stay interested than a girl's does. Channel surfing provides action, changes in noise level, and speed. Very few girls channel surf, not even during commercials. But for most guys it's a highly developed talent. In fact, in my house the males know just exactly how long they can channel surf during a commercial break before returning to whatever it is they were watching. It's like they have a television timing clock built into their biological systems. (They don't, by the way. It just seems like it.)

Speed, action, risk

Think for a minute about some of the most dangerous, risky, and fast professions in the world. Firefighter. Racecar driver. Fighter pilot. Boxer. Police officer. Explorer. Soldier. Most of these positions are filled by men. True, there are women in all of these professional fields. And any woman who wants to pursue a career in these areas should be given every opportunity to do so. But the fact remains that more men than women are attracted to dangerous, risky, and fast professions. Why?

"The hardest thing about being a teen guy is sitting still."

—Evan, 15

It's biological. It's testosterone. The same hormone that makes guys competitive also makes them more likely to take risks. In addition, there are certain chemicals in the brain that cause a person to avoid risk and danger. One of them, serotonin, can be compared to the brakes on a car. Guys have lower levels of serotonin than girls. In other words, they have less braking power. At the same time the chemical that works like the gas pedal in a car, dopamine, is produced in a part of the brain that's bigger in guys than girls. So not only do guys have low braking levels, but they also have high acceleration levels. All of that explains why many guys like to drive fast, like high-adventure sports, and like the challenge of trying to succeed at difficult tasks.

Boys like to pretend.
Matthew, age 7

Fighting and wrestling

When my husband has had a long day at work, and my junior high son has had a long day at school, and they both come home exhausted, tired, and hungry, it seems obvious to me that they should sit down, rest for a while, and grab something to eat. But instead when they walk in the back door and drop their backpack and briefcase on the floor, the first thing they do is wrestle.

> "The hardest thing about being a teen guy is having to be a stud and the pressure to be the strongest."
>
> —Drew, 17

When a group of college kids are reunited with their old high school friends, the girls hug each other, ask questions, talk about stuff, ooh and aah over new hairstyles, and say things like, "I missed you soooo much. I have so much to tell you. You look great. How's school? Did you hear that Sue and Jake broke up?" The guys wrestle.

> "The hardest thing about being a teen guy is dealing with everyone's sports expectations when you're not an athlete."
>
> —Mike, 17

When a group of elementary students is given free time on the playground, the girls jump rope, huddle up and talk, push each other on the swings, and giggle about the funny clothes the lunch lady is wearing. The boys wrestle.

Of course, it doesn't always happen this way, but it sure does happen a lot. Boys are rough-and-tumble kinds of people. When a guy wrestles his friend to the floor, it doesn't

 Someday I hope to meet a boy that I like and is cute and nice.
Emily, age 9

mean, "I hate you." It means, "It's so good to see you! How are you doing? Is school going okay? Do you like your new job? Nice car! Want to come over and watch the game tonight?"

"The hardest thing about being a guy today is trying to fit in with the stereotypical "guy" image."

—Luke, 16

It's true. Guys speak volumes when they engage in friendly physical aggression. It's a way of connecting with friends, rather than talking for hours on the phone like some girls do. It's a way of trying to become the leader in a group of friends. It's a way of burning off all the physical energy that builds up during boyhood and adolescence. And eventually, it happens less and less. Think about it. When you go to church with your parents, your dad doesn't wrestle his friends to the ground, does he?

No. At least I hope not.

Macho and in charge

"The hardest thing about being a teen guy is feeling like you always have to impress people when you really don't."

—Justin, 18

Almost every girl has thought to herself, "Why do guys always show off and try to act so macho?" In fact, this was one of the most asked questions on the surveys that students filled out for this book. Sometimes the wording was a

Boys interrupt a lot.
Madeleine, age 8

little different . . . "Why do guys try to act so tough? Why do guys think they're all that? Why do guys always have to be the best? Why do guys always want to be in charge?"

All of those questions mean the same thing. In the words of Ally, a junior in high school, "A guy starts to have a nice conversation with you when you're alone, but as soon as you add some friends into the equation, he gets all rude and once again starts ignoring you because he has to be the bomb."

Ah, yes. The Bomb. The Man. The Guy.

Honestly, girls, guys don't even realize they do this. As you keep reading, you're going to realize that so much of what you might consider "guy behavior" is interrelated and connected. For example, guys have a naturally competitive attitude. Their relationship groups have a "top dog," or leader. Those two things cause some guys to act macho in order to be seen as successful and powerful. It's true that acting successful and powerful isn't the same as being successful and powerful, but guys—and girls—often do things to create a public image that seems desirable.

"I think it's harder to be a guy than a girl because some of us are losers and will never fit in."

—Colt, 14

Guys are yearning to be men. And it won't be long before they reach that stage. In the meantime the macho act is one way that they begin expressing who they hope to someday become—a strong, courageous, and honorable man—because as teens many guys don't really feel that way. Guys feel a lot of pressure to be strong, tough, in

Boys like to marry girls.
Bryssa, age 4

charge, and "all that." Trust me, girls. The macho act will begin to fade away. If you can start viewing it as a step toward maturity, it might make a difference in how you see and relate to guys.

TO READ—

1 Samuel 17

Read the story of David and Goliath and notice the different ways the guys and men react to the situation around them.

TO THINK ABOUT—

1. Think about recent movies, television shows, sports events, news stories, etc. In what ways do they encourage or pressure guys to be tough and macho?

2. Has there ever been a time when you've been glad that a guy or man has acted tough or macho? What were the circumstances?

3. Do you think girls are pressured to act tough and macho? If so, how? If not, what other things are they pressured to be?

4. What difference do you think there is between "tough and macho" and "brave and strong"?

Girls take pictures at parties.
Lauren, age 3

LIST THREE THINGS
YOU DON'T UNDERSTAND
ABOUT GIRLS

"Why they all go to the bathroom together.
Why they get so uptight about everything.
Why they eat ice cream when they're sad."
—Ryley, 16

"Why they have to giggle all the time. Why they clog the
hallways all the time. The many pairs of shoes."
—Joseph, 17

"The bathroom thing. Why they need so many shoes.
Why they travel en masse most everywhere."
—Ben, 17

"Why they are so focused on material things and shopping.
Why they are always talking trash about other girls.
Why they can talk, cry, or flirt their way out of anything."
—Joe, 19

"Why they pack sooooo many shoes on a trip."
—Josh, 18

"Why they are so fickle."
—Jared, 15

"Why they write notes."
—Evan, 15

"Why they ask if an outfit makes them look fat. Why they use pens more often than pencils."
—Kyle, 14

"Why they can be so crabby. Why they remember all the little things. Why they change their mind."
—Jason, 15

"Why they like dangerous, rough guys."
—Justin, 18

"Why they are so dramatic."
—Devon, 15

"Tanning beds to get ready for the beach. The belts they wear that have no purpose and don't even go through the loops. Going to the bathroom in groups—there aren't even that many stalls usually, are there?"
—Bradford, 16

"Why they always play with their hair. Why then can talk on the phone for hours on end. How they can go to the malls for hours without buying anything."
—Daniel, 16

"Shopping. Shopping. Shopping."
—Erik, 17

"Whether they mean what they say. How they have time to put so much makeup and stuff on in the morning before school. Why they're so mean to each other."
—Josh, 17

"They like you Tuesday, but now it's Saturday!
They like guys who are tough and mean
rather than gentle and nice."
—Tyler, 13

"Why they cry over the simplest things."
—Michael, 13

"Why they love shoes."
—Eric, 13

"Why does it take a millennium to fix hair?"
—Ian, 14

"Why they change their mind all the time.
Why they are always mad at you.
Why they are always putting on lip gloss."
—Jacob, 12

"Why they always get into their huddle groups."
—Scott, 14

"Why they hold grudges for so long."
—Chris, 14

"Why does it take them so long to get dressed?"
—Paul, 14

"Why they always want to talk."
—Ryan, 13

"Why they freak out at mice.
Why they go to the bathroom in packs."
—Andrew, 14

"Clothes. The mall. Hair."
—Owen, 14

"Cheerleading. Makeup. Clothes."
—Chase, 12

"Why they toss their hair.
Why they giggle so much.
Why they say 'whatever.'"
—Adam, 12

"Why they are mean to me.
Why they are taller than me. Why they hurt me."
—Evan, 15

"Why they have to talk 100 miles an hour.
Why they take forever to get ready."
—Peter, 18

"Jealousy. Mind games. Obsessions."
—Brad, 18

Chapter 6

Boogers, Belches, and Bugs— Guys and Grossness

> **booger** *n* mucus from or in the nose, either green and gooey or green and crusty
>
> **belch** *v* to eject gas noisily from the stomach through the mouth, to eructate.
>
> > *n* an eructation
>
> **bug** *n* any terrestrial or aquatic insect with piercing, sucking mouth parts, wingless or with two pairs of wings, as the stinkbug, squash bug, or bedbug
>
> > *v* to annoy or bother

"Why do guys act so immature?"
    – Samantha, 17 – Christine, 14 – Brianna, 14 – Nicole, 16 – Stacy, 15 – Hanna, 15 – Steph, 15 – Carrie, 14 – Sammie, 16, etc.

Girls really like to be in clubs.
Lauren, age 5

"Guys are rude and gross."

—Amanda, 16

"I hate to say it, but guys can be pretty slobbish."

—Pastor Dave, 42

Fact: The female body and the male body both have the same digestive system.

Fact: The female body and the male body both have the same sinus drainage system.

Fact: The female body and the male body both produce digestive gasses, sometimes known as "burps" and "toots"

Fact: The female body and the male body both produce sinus mucus sometimes known as "snot" or "boogers."

"By the age of 17, most girls can function as adults, while the boys are still giving each other wedgies at the swimming pool and lighting farts."

—Barbara and Allan Pease, *Why Men Don't Talk and Women Can't Read Maps*

So why, then, does it seem like guys have the market on gross bodily fluids and gross bodily noises?

Almost every single girl who filled out the guy and girl survey for this book had these questions on their minds:

"Why are guys so gross? Why are guys so immature? Why do guys think stupid things are so funny? Why do guys laugh at dumb jokes? Why do guys think body noises are such a big deal?"

Those questions may not seem related at first glance, but read them again. Do you see a connection? Did you know that guys mature slower than girls? It's true. Teen guys are about one to two years less mature than teen girls. Since the word *immature* sounds so critical, let's use the words *less mature* to try to see how all those questions you just read are related.

—Teen guys are less mature than teen girls.

—Since teen guys are less mature than teen girls, things that seem childish or silly to the girls might seem funny to the boys.

—Since things like body noises, dumb jokes, and gross things are somewhat childish and silly, teen guys, who are less mature than teen girls, might think those things are funnier than teen girls do.

Do you see the connection?

"I used to think the why-don't-men-ask-for-directions question was the defining issue of the gender wars. Wrong. Body noises is the subject that truly polarizes us."

—*Mademoiselle* advice columnist, Blanche Vernon, as quoted in *A Return to Modesty*

Several years ago some scientists got together with some museum people who then got together with a writer named Sylvia Branzei, and they created something called "Grossology." It was a traveling science exhibit that was presented all over the United States, and here are some of the facts it presented:

Burps and toots are results of gas buildup in the body.

A toot is not a backward burp.

Boys like not-girl stuff more than girls.
Eden, age 4

Burping is officially known as "eructation."

Tooting does not have an official name. It is sometimes referred to as "farting," "passing gas," "breaking wind," "ripping one," and "cutting a puffy," among others.

"I wish girls understood that we are not dorks."

—Chase, 12

Burps originate in the stomach and result from excess air combined with digestive acids.

Toots originate in the large intestine and result from the gas that is produced by the bacteria that digests food.

People, both male and female, pass gas an average of 14 times a day.

Ants, by the way, do not burp.

Snot is produced when the mucus in your nose combines with bacteria-killing chemicals. Snot coats the tiny hairs in your noise, which then help trap the dirt you breathe, keeping it from getting into your lungs. You proceed to swallow the dirty snot throughout the day, and then it is destroyed in your stomach.

The nasal area of a human being is one of the cleanest areas of the body.

"I wish girls understood that guys just want to be immature sometimes."

—Mike, 17

On average, people, both male and female, manufacture and swallow about one quart (about one liter) of their own snot a day.

Girls do not like bugs.
Tanner, age 7

The act of nose picking is officially referred to as "rhinotillexomania."

Don't you feel smarter now?

> "The only bugs girls like are calapitters and butterflies."
>
> —Bryssa, 5

A few summers ago about 25 ninth graders from my town took a trip down to Chicago. On the second morning of the trip the male and female leaders were both sleep-deprived, exhausted, and haggard-looking. The male leader said to the female leader, "You look awful. What happened last night?" The female leader said, "The girls were up all night talking about boys, picking out their outfits for today, comparing their shoes, trading clothes, modeling their swim-suits for each other, painting their nails, plucking each other's eyebrows, telling stories, and doing their hair. I didn't get any sleep. You look awful, too. What happened to you?"

The male leader said, "I was up until four in the morning while the guys all tried to outfart one another. I didn't get any sleep, either, but I did have a few good laughs."

No one is able to say for sure why guys and girls have such a different viewpoint on body noises and function, but here are a few possibilities:

- Girls, as we said earlier, mature sooner than guys. But eventually the guys catch up. When was the last time your dad burped out loud at a restaurant? You see, they do grow out of it.

- Girls tend to be more inhibited because they have higher levels of the brain chemical serotonin, which

Boys love to chase girls.
Lauren, age 5

works like the brakes in a car. It's easier for girls to say to themselves, "My stomach is really churning right now. This could be a problem. What am I going to do? One thing's for sure. I'm not going to do anything in public that might be embarrassing."

- The part of the brain that keeps a person interested and attentive is less sensitive in guys than girls, so they get bored more easily. When they get bored, they often start acting up, wiggling, being silly, etc. In a girl's brain the "thinking" part more easily overrides the "reacting" part than it does in a guy's brain.

"I swear . . . their brains are smaller than a pea."

—Corin, 15

One of the problems with understanding guys during the teenage years is that their bodies often look mature, but their brains aren't quite at the same developmental level. In other words, their bodies are grown, but their brains aren't. Because of that the mantra of many teen girls when they're with teen guys is, "Would you just grow up already?!"

Actually, some girls start saying this as early as kindergarten when boys have been known to pull on a girl's braids as a way to get her attention, to chew up his food and then display it to the entire class on the tip of his tongue, or to pick his nose and then promptly consume whatever it is that's dangling from the tip of his finger.

Television commercials and sitcoms often make it seem like guys never grow out of the less mature stage. The media seems determined to portray guys both young and old as immature, childish, silly, sports-fanatical, car-crazy, toy-loving creatures who, like Peter Pan, never grow up. And it must be good for sales; otherwise the media would stop doing it.

"Why do guys have farting contests to impress each other?"

—Amy, 16

The fact is, however, that there are lots of teenage guys who never burp in public, never tell silly jokes, aren't interested in gross things, and act rather mature for their age. If there are 15 guys and 15 girls in a high school class, and if only two or three of the guys act immature and love to make body noises in public, the 15 girls will usually define the entire teenage male population as "immature, disgusting, and gross" based on those few individuals.

Likewise, if only two or three of the girls in the class talk nonstop about shopping, gossip about other people, and don't know how to change a tire on their cars, the 15 boys will usually define the entire teenage female population as "backbiting, shopaholic ditzes" based on those few individuals.

"Boys like lots of material things (remote control cars, TV's, motorcycles, etc.)"

—Madeleine, 8

Not only do girls often broadly categorize all guys as gross and immature, but they also tend to forget that many members of their own gender fit the same description. I had three roommates in college who could beat any guy in a burping contest. I've been in cars and buses and classrooms

Girls do odd things that I don't understand.
Joshua, age 10

with girls who could clear out a football stadium with the body sounds and smells they produced. And I've been at sleepovers with senior high girls who giggle and laugh and whisper and tell secrets just like third graders.

"Boys definitely burp and fart more than girls. Especially the really immature ones. Not us, of course."

—Tate, 12 and Charlie, 11

The biggest difference between the gross level of guys and girls is that girls tend not to brag about their skills. Guys, you may remember, are very competitive. So of course, if there are gross body noises being discussed, there will naturally be a contest to see who's best . . . or worst, as the case may be. A guy may congratulate his friend on a magnificent burp, but he will then immediately proceed to try and outburp him. A girl, on the other hand, will probably just congratulate her friend and leave it at that.

"Why do guys act like they're...

...2nd graders?"   —Molly, 15

...seven years old?"   —Erika, 14

...five years old?"   —Tabitha, 14

Another thing to keep in mind is that, for as long as anyone can remember, society has looked to females to be genteel, refined, and polite. That's not to say that people expected males to be the opposite. Rather they expected that the gentle and refined politeness of females would encourage males to follow suit. Does it really work this way?

Boys don't like to listen to important things.
Madeleine, age 8

That's a little hard to say. Certainly, if a guy has a crush on a girl and he finds out that she thinks burping is disgusting, he might change his behavior, at least when he's in her presence. Then again he might decide he's not quite ready to give up this exciting pastime and that girls can wait for a while. Truly, girls, this issue is a bit of a mystery, even to the guys themselves.

I met with a group of guys (all different ages) and told them that girls didn't understand why guys thought body noises and silly things and gross stuff and childish behavior were such a big deal. The guys laughed, pushed each other around a little bit, joked, and then one of them burped. Loudly.

> "Guys are loud, obnoxious, and say dumb things."
>
> —Cherline, 16

Then I asked them if they could tell me why so many guys did those things, and they were at a loss for words. "I don't know." "Just because it's fun, I guess." "We just do, that's all." Those were as precise as the answers got. One senior guy said, "It's just something we do, but as we get older, we stop. Or at least we do it less." And then I noticed that it was mostly the younger guys who were acting silly and trying to burp the alphabet. The older guys were considerably more polite.

This difference in age behavior showed up in the guy and girl surveys. The younger guys who filled out the survey often wrote down sarcastic, silly, ridiculous answers. For example, one young guy gave these answers—

 When boys are mad they don't talk to the person they are mad at.
Emily, age 9

> *Name some things that guys (in general) are better at than girls:* Everything
>
> *Name some things that girls (in general) are better at than guys:* Nothing.

Another young guy gave these answers—

> *Name some things that guys (in general) are better at than girls:* spitting, burping, farting, going to the bathroom standing up.
>
> *Name some things that girls (in general) are better at than guys:* cooking, cleaning, having babies, being crabby, being annoying.

 "Why do guys always make disgusting body noises?"

—Hannah, 14

Many of the older guys, on the other hand, seemed to have more thoughtful and honest answers. One older teen guy wrote:

> *Name some things that guys (in general) are better at than girls:* I don't know . . . some are better at sports. Some aren't. Some are better at mechanical things. Some aren't. It all depends. I do think we're better at letting go of a problem or conflict once it's over with.
>
> *Name some things that girls (in general) are better at than guys:* I think girls are really good at building close friendships. They understand relationships better than guys, I think. They're also better at understanding and relating to other people's feelings.

 Girls like Barbies.
Alyssa, age 7

Can you see the difference between these answers? Clearly, as guys get older, their maturity starts to become apparent. It just arrives a little bit later than it does for most girls.

So what can you do about a guy whose immaturity is starting to really get you down? I think it's very appropriate for girls to let a guy know if he's doing something that's rather impolite. If a guy walks up to you, makes a crude joke, and then laughs, you have every right to say, "You know, I don't really appreciate that at all. Please don't talk to me that way." That's going to accomplish much more than saying, "You jerk. You're so stupid. Why don't you just grow up and stop being such an animal." If you say something like that, he might just laugh and think, "Wow, that was awesome! Maybe if I do the same thing tomorrow, she'll scream and make a girly scene."

> "It's so annoying when one of them farts and the others all laugh and congratulate him."
>
> —Lauren, 14

In the end, girls, this is what it comes down to:

• Not all guys are gross, disgusting slobs who think boogers are for bouncing, bugs are for smashing, and burps are for communicating.

• The guys in your school (or family or church) whom you consider to be "immature, gross, disgusting slobs" probably still have some maturing to do. Be patient.

• The fact that you are annoyed by some guys' behavior doesn't make you better or superior. Nor does it give you a right to trash guys.

Girls like to play tennis.
Bryssa, age 4

• Most guys grow up to be decent and kind men . . . even the ones who, right now, think it's cool to make fake farting sounds by sticking one hand under their armpit and then pumping their elbow up and down really fast.

• No one asked you to be the politepolice. If you are a well-mannered, mature young woman, good for you. The world needs more people like that. But let your behavior be your example to others instead of resorting to lecturing, eye-rolling, tsk-tsking, and the ever famous, "Just grow up, will you!?"

TO READ—

Proverbs 13:20

TO THINK ABOUT—

1. Do you think the girls or guys in your grade act more mature? Why?

2. In what ways have you noticed guys your age maturing over the past few years?

3. Think of some examples of commercials that portray guys as being dumb, immature slobs. How do you react when you see these? Why do you think advertisers portray guys like this?

4. Why do people think body noises are ruder coming from a girl than from a guy?

Girls like to smell flowers.
Lauren, age 3

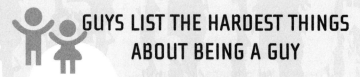

GUYS LIST THE HARDEST THINGS ABOUT BEING A GUY

(Top answers—school, lust, peer pressure)

Not having money.
—Ryley,16

Finding a girl who understands you.
—Jason, 16

The expectation to be good at sports.
—Mike, 17

Living up to other people's standards.
—Joseph, 17

Trying to keep your own identity and your own code.
—Ben, 17

Temptation.
—Erik, 18

Homework
—Joe, 16

Getting along with parents.
—Joe, 19

Peer pressure.
—Nate, 18

Making the right choices.
—Josh, 18

Pressure to do things and not wimp out.
—Mark, 16

Trying to follow God in a world
where Satan tries to bring you down.
—Stephen, 17

Having to be a "stud," having to be the strongest, being
thought of by others as only thinking of sex.
—Drew, 17

Being emotionally hurt by girls.
—Ty, 18

Being accepted.
—Jared, 15

Doing surveys like this.
—Mike, 15

Growing a mullet.
—Jake, 15

Sitting still.
—Nick, 15

Trying to fit in.
—Luke, 16

Lust . . . it's hard to remain pure in the world we live in.
—Justin, 19

Competition.
—Brad, 18

Being accepted.
—Danny, 19

Dealing with the temptations and lust.
Television ads try to appeal to the sexual part of guys.
Sex sells is the theme of everything.
—A.J., 18

Thinking you have to live up to some macho image.
It takes a lot to let go of your ego and rely on God.
—Rob, 18

Lust—the way girls dress and act in today's society
invites our minds to wander.
—Ian, 18

Lust—the struggle to see a girl for who she is,
not what she wears.
—Matt, 19

Being around girls who dress and act scandalously.
There's always been a problem with lust with guys,
but the girls aren't doing anything to help us.
—Josh, 17

Trying to fit in.
—Keyle, 13

Getting on the school sports team.
—Aaron, 14

The influence of girls' skimpy clothing.
—Michale, 13

Trying to be popular.
—Corey, 13

Algebra.
—Chris, 14

Being called a dork.
—Chase, 12

Being "cool."
—Trevor, 12

Being short.
—Evan, 15

Staying out of trouble.
—Travis, 13

Always being in trouble.
—Joe, 15

Resisting alcohol and drugs.
—David, 17

Being yourself.
—Peter, 18

Chapter 7

Babble, Banter, and Ballhyoo—

Guys and Words

---

babble *v* to utter unintelligibly, to blurt out; tell thoughtlessly or foolishly; to utter inarticulate sounds or meaningless noises; to talk unwisely or foolishly

banter *n* good-humored ridicule, repartee

ballyhoo *n* noisy patter; conspicuous noisiness of speech, manner, or habit

---

"What do girls really mean when they tell you things . . . nothing never means nothing when a girl says it."

> —A.J., 18

"Something that bothers me about girls? Incessant talking!"

> —Scott, 17

Boys are lazy.
Madeleine, age 8

"Why do girls talk on the phone so much?"

—Trevor, 12

"Put simply, males have limited abilities when it comes to speech and conversation."

—Pease, *Why Men Don't Talk and Women Can't Read Maps*

Several years ago I was chaperoning the high school prom in my town. About halfway through the evening I made a trip to the girls' bathroom (by myself). On the way there I passed by seven guys who were sitting in lounge chairs. Their tux jackets were either unbuttoned or draped over the chair arms. Their legs were sprawled out in front of them. Their eyes were glazed over, probably from too many flash photos and really uncomfortable shoes. Most noticeable of all they were, all seven of them, silent. They seemed to be having a fine time hanging out together in a row without saying a word.

"I wish girls understood that guys just don't care as much about intricate details."

—Erik, 18

When I got to the girls' bathroom and walked in, I saw the dates of the seven silent guys. They were all in the bathroom together. Some were flocked around the mirrors, checking on their hairstyles and reapplying lip gloss. Some were using the sinks to try to rinse red punch out of their dresses. Some were readjusting their panty hose. One was crying about something her boyfriend had said to her. Another one was trying to comfort the crying girl. A third one was plotting revenge on the nasty boyfriend. All seven girls were talking. They seemed to be having a fine time together hanging out in the bathroom and bonding through the miracle of conversation.

The subject of communication—how to use it, lack of it, what it is—is one that will exist between males and females for as long as they both shall live. Most guys complain that girls talk too much, and most girls complain that guys talk too little (except in the case of talking when they're not supposed to, like in class, and then girls seem to think that guys talk too much). Countless books have been written for adult men and women on "how to communicate," "how to talk so men will listen," "how to listen so men will talk," "how to know what your spouse is really saying," and "how to be a fabulous listener." But if males and females could just understand how their brains affect the way they talk—or don't talk, in some cases—then we'd all be better communicators, guaranteed.

> "You really don't need a whole lot of words to hit a buffalo in the head, but you do need a lot of words to teach children, to tell stories, to spread news, and to talk about the men."
>
>
>
> —Helen Fisher, anthropologist, from Discovery Channel's *Science of the Sexes* on why women talk more than men do

We've already talked about the fact that the female brain is very strong in the language area, and the male brain is very strong in the spatial area. That doesn't mean that all girls talk a lot and that all guys don't talk a lot. But certainly there are some very obvious differences between how girls and guys talk, why girls and guys talk, and when girls and guys talk.

Boys like superheroes.
Sage, age 6

How

From the time they're very young guys and girls talk to one another differently. In study after study with people of all different ages, it's been shown that females tend to sit closer to one another when they talk, they tend to face each other when they talk, and they make eye contact throughout a conversation. Guys, however, tend to keep more distance between them when talking. They also tend to stand in a more side-by-side position rather than facing one another. And they don't make eye contact nearly as much as girls do.

Because of these differences, when a guy and girl are having a conversation, girls often feel that the guy is ignoring her. If he stands far away, doesn't face her, and doesn't look her in the eye, a girl might think to herself, "He doesn't care about what I'm saying at all," when in fact, the guy is simply doing what he usually does.

And the guy might feel like the girl is purposely trying to make him uncomfortable by standing so close, facing him head-on, and looking him in the eye. "What is she doing? She's in my space! I gotta get out of here!"

"I wish girls understood that we're not mad just because we don't want to talk all the time."

—Daniel, 18

Another issue regarding how guys and girls talk has to do with nonverbal communication. Guys are very good at using nonverbal "words" to talk to other guys. Think about things like high-fives, head nods, and special handshakes. Have you noticed guys using these things to "talk" to one another?

Boys have short hair.
Eden, age 4

Last year I was welcoming kids to the youth group that I work with. A new guy walked in the door, and I went up to greet him. I asked his name, how old he was, and how he'd heard about the group. He said, "My friend told me about it at school today." This kid was what some people might call an outsider. A cruel person might refer to him as a "loser." I was curious to find out who had invited him, so I said, "Do you see your friend here?"

"Guys just do not communicate well."

—Tanya, 18

He looked around the room for a few moments and finally spotted the face he was looking for. He pointed to a guy in the far corner and said, "There he is." A girl might have waved and said "hi" and run over to her friend. But not this guy. He lifted his arm and gave what I call the "guy wave," a sort of quick motion with the hand that means, "Hey, how are you? Glad to see you. How was your day? I'm really looking forward to tonight. Thanks for inviting me, man." All of that with just a quick flick of the wrist.

The guy who'd invited him saw the "guy wave" and responded with what I call the "guy nod." He raised his chin ever so slightly, looked at his friend, and then did a little up-down toss of his head that said, "Hey, glad you came. Hope you didn't get lost on your way over here. You're going to have a great time tonight. I promise. If you want to come over here and hang out with me, that'd be cool." All of that with just a quick flick of the neck.

Just for the record, girls, guys do talk and communicate. They just sometimes do it differently than you do.

Girls usually have dolls.
Tanner, age 7

When they wrestle each other, knock each other around, bump into one another, and make slight movements with their heads, arms, shoulders and hands, they're talking. When they joke around with each other, sometimes even calling each other names, they're expressing their friendship. What might sound like adversarial bluster to you might in fact be friendly banter.

Guys and girls have different ways of talking and communicating. Don't forget it.

"I don't understand why guys won't talk about anything except cars, girls, and school."

—Janel, 18

Why

Another big difference between guys and girls is due to the reasons they communicate and talk. For guys talking is mostly about sharing information with each other. Deborah Tannen, a woman who's spent years studying the communication skills of people, calls it "report talk." A phone conversation between two guys might consist of nothing more than, "We're watching a movie at Jim's house at nine tonight. Bring some money for pizza. See ya." Notice how much was communicated in less than 20 words:

who—we

what—watching a movie

where—Jim's house

"I don't understand why guys won't listen to us when we talk."

—Christine, 18

 Boys don't really care about the fish's feelings when it gets hooked.
Lauren, age 5

when—nine tonight

why—because there will be pizza

extra pertinent info—bring some money.

If a girl wanted to communicate the same amount of information, she could potentially spend several hours on the phone. Why? Because for girls talking is not just about relaying information. It's also about building intimacy. Words, for girls, are a bonding tool. Conversation is not merely an exchange of information. It is a way to share oneself with another person. Guys have "report talk," and girls have "rapport talk." Rapport, for those of you who aren't sure, has to do with relationships between people who have a lot in common and who are closely connected to each other.

> "Girls are definitely better at communicating."
>
> —Kalena, 17

Many guys prefer to build rapport with one another by doing something rather than by talking. I know several sophomore guys who can spend hours watching television together—in silence—as a way to bond and strengthen their friendship. Some guys might feel closer to friends after spending an afternoon golfing, biking, or jamming on their guitars without actually ever speaking to one another.

I know it's hard to believe this, but most guys are pretty content to live a life of few words, few conversations, and absolutely no heart-to-heart talks.

Girls wear dresses with butterflies and butterfly shoes and boys wear cool clothes such as Hot Wheels shirts and Lego shirts.

Austen, age 6

When

There is one very specific time throughout their lives when guys tend to speak: when it's absolutely necessary. If non-verbal communication won't do the job, if hanging out together in silence won't do the job, and if there's no special handshake, head nod, or body slam that will do the job, then a guy will talk. A guy also might talk if a teacher says, "Okay, I don't want any talking for the next 15 minutes." Girls, however, will whisper in that situation.

When do girls talk? Whenever the opportunity arises. And if there isn't an opportunity readily available, then girls will create one. This is why girls go to the bathroom in groups. It provides yet another opportunity to talk, to bond, to share secrets, to solve life's crises, and to discuss what they should talk about next.

"Girls are way better than guys at expressing themselves."

—Jessica 16

There is a very good explanation for this difference between guys and girls. Each day guys speak between 2,000 and 4,000 words. They make between 1,000 and 2,000 communication sounds (uh-huh, mmm, eh?, etc.). And they make between 2,000 and 3,000 nonverbal communication actions, such as hand gestures and facial expressions. If you add all those numbers together, you'll see that guys "speak" between 5,000 and 9,000 "words" per day.

Girls, however, speak between 6,000 and 8,000 words, make between 2,000 and 3,000 sounds, and between 8,000 and 10,000 communication actions. Add them all up, and girls "speak" between 16,000 and 21,000 "words" per day. In other words, girls—on average—speak anywhere between three and four times as many "words" each day as guys do.

> "Why won't guys just say what's on their mind?"
>
> —Jessica, 16

It's impossible to decide whether girls speak more often because they have more words to say each day, or if girls speak more words each day because they speak more often. That's the "which came first, the chicken or the egg" question in the female world. Not that it makes much difference. Girls (most of them) talk more than guys (most of them), and nothing is going to change that.

In a crisis situation guys are more likely to jump to action, and girls are more likely to jump to communication. Do you remember what happened when the angel visited Mary and told her that she was going to give birth to God's son? She immediately headed over to her cousin's house and told her all about it. She shared every detail. And then she wrote a poem about it. She needed to tell someone what was going on in her life.

> "I don't understand why guys hate talking on the phone."
>
> —Chelsea, 17

Joseph, on the other hand, reacted to the angel's visit very differently. He woke up, thought about things for a while, wrestled with the situation privately, and then proceeded to do exactly what the angel had told him to. And as far as we know, the two of them got along just fine, which means that it's very possible for guys and girls to move beyond the talking issue and have a meaningful relationship.

Girls like to pick up "calepitters."
Bryssa, age 4

Because girls can use both sides of their brain at once, girls can talk and do something else. In fact, a girl's brain can create language on both sides whereas a guy's creates language only on the left side. So not only do girls have a higher quantity of words each day, but they also have a higher quality of words, meaning that their language skills, in general, are better developed than those of guys.

"I don't understand why guys won't look at you when they talk."

—Paula, 16

Why is it important to know this? So that you understand these things—

If a guy isn't talking to you, it doesn't mean he's mad at you.

If a guy doesn't seem to be listening to you, it might be because he's doing something else and can only focus on one thing at a time.

If a guy doesn't look you in the eye during a conversation, it doesn't mean he's daydreaming or ignoring you.

If a guy gives you the "guy nod" or the "guy wave," he's talking to you.

If you want to have a conversation with a guy, it might be best to find some kind of activity that you both enjoy and can do together. Then, when there's a break in the action, strike up a conversation. Don't expect him to do and talk at the same time.

Finally, remember that all the tiny details are not important to most guys. If you have something to say or a story to tell, keep it short and to the point. Save all those extra words for your next girl-group trip to the bathroom

Girls like to pick up phones to call people.
Lauren, age 3

or your next phone conversation. Your girl friends will be happy that you did and so will your guy friends. In the end it's possible for everyone to be happy and pleasant if you just remember that words are a girl's—but probably not a guy's—best friend.

TO READ—

Proverbs 10:19, 12:18, 16:24, 17:27, 18:6-7

TO THINK ABOUT—

1. Do you have any guy friends who are easy to talk to? What kinds of things do you talk about? Why is it easy to communicate with him?

2. Why do you think it's so much easier (in general) for girls to talk to each other than for guys to talk to each other?

3. What are both some good and bad things about a person who doesn't talk much?

4. What are both some good and bad things about a person who talks a lot?

Boys are affectionate with their mothers, but not other girls, until they are about 16 years old.

Tanner, age 7

GUYS THINK
GUYS ARE BETTER AT . . .

spitting

keeping friends

everything

mechanics

hunting

saying what they mean

sports

manual labor

working with their hands

athletics

rational thinking

logic

not overreacting

keeping secrets

driving

lifting weights

lifting heavy objects

video games

common sense

fixing things

building things

wrestling, baseball, football, cars

being in the army

technology

playing drums

fighting

playing guitar

dirt biking

being carefree

handling problems

shopping quickly

getting over stuff

forgiveness

decision making

courage

resolving differences

skateboarding

bodybuilding

being less preppy

computers

fishing

staying calm

hiding their feelings

Chapter 8

Bumps, Bruises, and Blues— Guys and Emotions

bump *n* a violent impact or collision

bruise *n* a surface injury caused by violent contact

      v to injure, to hurt or offend, as feelings

blue *adj* feeling downcast or depressed, experiencing melancholy

"I wish girls understood how much effect they have on our self-esteem and not to abuse that influence."

    —Joe, 19

"I wish girls would understand that we are sensitive people as well."

    —Ben, 17

Girls feel sad when a deer gets killed.
Lauren, age 5

"It's pretty hurtful when someone tells me that something I do doesn't measure up."

—A.J., 18

It was in the summer of 2002 that Christian died in a car accident. He'd just graduated from high school, and his college plans were all neatly laid out. He'd been a varsity swimmer and had a smile that could charm an entire crowd. All throughout high school he'd been in the youth group I help with, and never once had I seen him walk through the door without a grin on his face.

"I don't understand why girls are so emotional and why they take stuff so seriously."

—Nathaniel, 13

During the funeral visitation Christian's closest friend, Bryan, was off by himself. Every once in a while someone would go over and say something to him or try to get him to talk. But Bryan remained silent and stoic. Sometimes he paced back and forth. Sometimes he stopped still in his tracks and seemed to be staring off into another world. Always he seemed distant and lost in his thoughts.

At some point Mark and I noticed that Bryan was gone. No one had noticed him leave. No one knew where he'd headed or where to look for him. My immediate reaction was worry and fear. "Do you think we should try to find him and make sure he's okay?" I asked Mark. "He just needs to be alone for a while," was Mark's response. "The only thing we can do is wait. He'll be back when he's ready."

Boys like tools.
Sage, age 6

Amy, another of Christian's close friends, reacted in a completely different manner. She'd been quietly crying throughout the afternoon, hugging her friends, looking at the pictures of Christian that were displayed in the hallway, and openly talking about how sad and upset and angry and hurt she was. As the afternoon wore on, she became more and more agitated and emotional. Eventually, she had to be driven home by some friends because she couldn't handle the pain and sorrow any longer.

Amy and Bryan both loved Christian.

They both grieved over his death.

They both had deep, deep feelings of sadness, confusion, anger, and pain.

But they expressed and dealt with those feelings very differently, in part because they are two distinct individuals, but also because one is a girl and one is a guy.

"I wish girls understood that we're not so emotional."

—Michael, 13

The subject of guys and emotions is confusing to girls in two different ways. First, most girls are confused by how guys deal with their own emotions. Because many girls are so open about their feelings and because many guys are so private about their feelings, girls often feel frustrated and confused. Why won't guys talk about how they're feeling? Do they ever feel sad? Why don't they cry? Why do they want to be alone when they're upset?

Second, most girls are confused—or upset—about how guys deal with other people's emotions. Why don't they

Boys like lizards.
Eden, age 4

care about how I feel? Why don't they ask what's wrong? Why won't they try to understand what I'm going through? Why are they so insensitive?

> "Girls are definitely better at expressing their emotions."
>
> —Daniel, 16

These are the questions hundreds of girls asked about guys and emotions. By the way, hundreds of guys asked similar questions about girls. Why do they cry so much? Why do they turn every little thing into a big deal? Why can't they just get over things quickly? Why do they always want to talk about how they're feeling? Why do they pressure us to talk about how we're feeling?

So you see, girls, the confusion runs in both directions. Let's see if we can help clear things up at least a little bit.

Guys and their own emotions

First of all let's make sure one thing is very clear—guys do have feelings. They do have emotions. They do know about happiness, sadness, anger, sorrow, fear, and pain. I know this is true for two reasons. First, guys have told me. And second, the greatest example of humanity, Jesus, experienced all those things. He was sad when the rich young ruler decided not to follow him. He was angry when he saw how the merchants were using the temple as a place of business. He was happy when little children wanted to be with him. He was afraid of the pain that went along with dying. He was excited about being with his heavenly Father once again.

Girls like to eat Jello and pudding.
Tanner, age 7

The biggest difference between guys and girls isn't the emotions themselves, but rather how they deal with those emotions. Here are two observations girls have made about guys and emotions: They don't talk about how they're feeling, and they don't cry in front of other people.

"I wish girls understood that guys deal with emotions differently."

—Jacob, 15

Of course, you've probably all known at least a few guys who do talk about how they're feeling and who do cry in front of other people. And you've probably all known at least a few girls (maybe you're like this) who don't like to talk about how they're feeling and who don't like to cry in front of other people. But for the most part those two statements are true of most guys.

"Guys are better than girls at hiding their feelings."

—Justin, 19

You might remember that in the brain chapter we talked a little bit about how a guy's brain processes emotions. First, a guy's brain deals with emotions only on the right side. As with most other things in a guy's brain emotions are dealt with in a very focused way, meaning most guys can't deal with their emotions plus something else. Guys tend to "mono-task"—do one thing at a time— because of how their brain functions. So if a guy has a very emotional experience while he's at school or work, he'll probably store it away until later when he can give it his full attention.

Boys can be really nice, but not usually.
Lauren, age 5

Lots of people think that guys are ignoring or hiding their feelings when this happens, but they're really just dealing with things according to their biological design. Some guys will use the stored strength of those emotions later on. Let me give you an example. If a guy is on a football team that has big game coming up, and if someone from the other team does something to make the guy angry, the first guy can store that anger away and then use it during the game to give him more energy, more drive, or more determination to win. Or if a guy has a lead role in the school musical, and some macho, tough, stud wannabe teases him about being involved in the arts, the first guy can put that anger away in his brain and either deal with it later or use it as a boost during a performance.

On average, scientists say that guys often wait seven hours before dealing with strong emotions. That's because most guys don't view emotions as something to experience and analyze and share with their friends. Instead they view them as problems to be solved. They don't use their pain or sorrow to bond or draw close to their friends like many girls do. They either try to "solve" it, "fix" it, or use it to their advantage.

"I wish girls understood that we have feelings, too."

—James, 15

Guys get two very mixed messages from society. On the one hand they're told to be tough and strong, never to appear weak, never to let anyone see them cry. On the other hand they're told to "get in touch with their emotions," "not to be afraid to let them see you cry," to "let their softer side show." What a confusing situation to be stuck in! I think

Girls like to sit around and say, "I'm so bored."
Joshua, age 10

that girls need to respect the fact that guys don't usually deal with their emotions the same way girls do. Girls shouldn't try to push guys to open up and talk about things if they don't want to. Girls shouldn't assume that guys are unfeeling just because it might appear that way on the outside. And when a guy does show weakness or sorrow or pain, girls should never, ever tease them about it.

"I feel like crying."
—Charlie Brown, after losing yet another baseball game

Guys do feel pain, especially when others refer to them in ways that cut them down. I asked guys to list the most hurtful things that other people call them. Here are just a few:

wuss
gay
fag
loser
dork

One guy answered this way: "Any name or word that breaks the heart is hurtful, and this page isn't big enough to write them all."

All of those words listed above—and believe me, there are lots more—are totally demeaning and painful. Please, girls, don't ever call a guy, or girl, anything nasty, not even in a joking manner. You'll never know how much damage it may cause.

I'll be honest. After 20 years of marriage and 18 years of mothering boys, I still don't completely understand guys and their emotions. It can be pretty challenging to let my

Boys are different from girls because they don't paint their fingernails.
Emily, age 9

husband and sons deal with emotions in their own ways. Sometimes I wish guys wanted to talk about things the way girls do. Sometimes I wish guys would admit that they're scared, lonely, or sad. But there are just as many times when I'm very glad that God made guys the way he did. I'm glad that I can count on Mark to balance my areas of weakness with his areas of strength and vice versa. I'm glad that there are men and women who will put their fear aside in order to fight fires and chase criminals. I'm glad that when one person is weak, there's usually another person who is strong, and together they can face another day.

"I think in a lot of ways it's harder to be a guy. They don't always know how to act, and it's socially unacceptable for them to show their feelings."

—Ruby, 17

There's a reason God made men and women the way he did. It's so we'd be able to help one another, support one another, and encourage one another. Nowhere is that more obvious than when dealing with the power of emotions.

Guys and other people's emotions

Okay, so guys deal with their own emotions differently than girls do. Most girls can accept that. But it's not as easy to accept the way that guys deal with other people's emotions . . . especially ours. If he wants to "ignore" his own sadness and deal with it later, fine. But we certainly don't want him to ignore our sadness!

Part of the challenge in understanding how guys see others' emotions stems from the fact that girls see others'

Girls like to kiss boys.
Bryssa, age 4

emotions in a very unique way. Most females are what I call hypersensitive. Except for sight all of a girl's senses are more heightened and more acute than those of a guy. Her senses of taste, smell, touch, and hearing are very acute. That means that girls are often aware of what's going on in other people's lives. Girls might be able to hear a slight change in someone's voice that indicates sorrow or fear or excitement. Or they might be able to tell from the way their friends hug them that something is terribly wrong.

"Why do guys say nothing's wrong when something obviously is?"

—Nikki, 17

Because guys don't have the same intuitive abilities, we sometimes call them insensitive. But it's not really fair to compare a guy's sensitivity to a girl's because they're working with two different levels of sensory awareness. It might be fair to say that a guy's behavior may appear to be less sensitive than a girl's. But it's not fair to say that since a guy is less sensitive than a girl, then he must be insensitive.

"Guys don't take a simple problem and make it all complicated like girls do."

—Shannon, 16

There's another significant difference between guys and girls. Girls are easily able to recognize different emotions on other people's faces. It takes very little effort for a girl to sense how someone is feeling based simply on her facial expression. If you add that to a girl's heightened senses, you can see that it's very easy for most girls to know how others are feeling.

 Girls like to play on the computer with CDs on.
Lauren, age 3

Guys, on the other hand, have a much harder time reading other people's faces. They have to use a much larger portion of their brain to figure out the emotions that lie behind a facial expression. It is literally and biologically exhausting for a guy to try to understand what someone else is feeling. For that reason girls tend to be more empathetic than guys. It is much easier for a girl to put herself in someone else's shoes and feel what that person is feeling. That might be why so many girls are drawn to careers that deal with people. However, there are also lots of guys who become counselors, pastors, nurses, and other things that are people-oriented.

"Guys aren't very consoling or sympathetic to girls' problems."

—Janel, 18

In one very specific way guys are more understanding that you might realize. One of the survey questions asked, "Do you think it's harder to be a guy or a girl in today's society and why?" Almost all the girls said life was harder for them for a variety of reasons. Now if guys were really as insensitive and uncaring as girls sometimes think they are, you might expect that they would all answer that life was harder for them, right?

Wrong. Almost all the guys said they thought life was harder for girls than guys.

"Girls face a lot of pressure to look a certain way."

"It seems like girls are always expected to look nice and to act right."

"Girls have to deal with all kinds of emotional stuff that I could never handle."

Boys like to play army.
Tanner, age 7

"Girls have to figure out the whole career and family thing, and sometimes they have to make choices and sacrifices."

"Sometimes it seems like girls still don't get the same respect as guys."

Do those statements sound like they were made by insensitive, uncaring people? I don't think so. Underneath it all I think guys have a fairly good understanding of pain, fear, sadness, and other emotions. But they approach and handle them differently. And that's okay, isn't it? If girls are really as sensitive and caring as we like to think we are, then we shouldn't have a problem letting guys deal with their emotions in their own way.

TO READ—

Psalm 38 (written by a man, by the way . . .)

TO THINK ABOUT—

1. Think about a time when you've known a guy was struggling with sadness, loneliness, disappointment, etc. How did he act? How did you respond?

2. Do you think guys are afraid to show emotions? Why, or why not?

3. Have you ever seen a guy being ridiculed for crying? What happened? How did you react?

4. Why do you think many people label guys as "insensitive" and "uncaring"?

Girls love to find really cool rocks.
Lauren, age 5

GUYS THINK
GIRLS ARE BETTER AT . . .

(Top answers—school, makeup, fashion, emotions, talking)

staying clean
using makeup
sitting still
talking
expressing emotions
being sociable
working with children
creativity
organization
singing
forming deep friendships
shopping
gossip
looking good
writing
social skills
doing 10 things at once
art
dressing nice
keeping in packs
talking on the phone
matching outfits

cheerfulness
showing feelings
studying
braiding hair
filling out surveys
keeping conversations going
compassion
love
staying calm
sensing what people are feeling
forming cliques
school
hygiene
homework
cheerleading
soccer
fashion
being mature
dancing
gymnastics
cooking
smelling good
tennis
softball
being outgoing
flirting

Chapter 9

Birds, Bees, and Babes— Guys and Sex

> **birds** *n pl* warm-blooded, feathered, egg-laying vertebrate having the forelimbs modified as wings
>
> **bees** *n pl* any of a large number of hymenopterous insects of the family Apoidea, solitary or social in habit, with smooth or hairy bodies, variously colored, and feeding largely upon nectar and pollen
>
> **birds and bees** *n* a colloquial expression for anything having to do with the reproductive life of human beings, sometimes referred to as "the facts of life"
>
> **babes** *n pl* infants, babies; colloquially an attractive male or female, also sometimes referred to as "hunk," "fox," "hottie," and other silly things

 did you know... Other than brain cells 50 million cells in a human's body will die and be replaced while reading this sentence. **?**

"Why do guys act one way around girls and then change when their friends show up?"

—All girls, all ages

"Why do guys care so much about how a girl's body looks?"

—Kiki, 16

"Why do guys always talk about sex?"

—Megan, 15

I vividly remember the first time I fell in love.

I was five years old.

I attended kindergarten at Devonshire Elementary School in the Chicago suburbs, and there was a boy in my class whose hair was parted neatly each day, who wore nice shirts to school (often buttoned all the way to the top of his neck), who wore brown leather lace-up shoes, who didn't talk a whole lot, and who smelled like soap. His mother must have been a woman who diligently washed behind her son's ears every day before he left the house because the soapy smell lingered around his presence every single morning that he walked into the classroom.

"Why do guys talk about a girl's chest size?"

—Ashley, 15

I'm not sure if was the neat way he dressed, his shyness, or the clean smell, but on the first day of school I promptly fell deeply in love with that little boy . . . whose name I can't remember anymore.

I realize that five-year-olds can't really understand romantic love. They understand parental love. They understand grandparental love. They understand about loving stuffed animals and loving a special toy and loving to dip everything they eat into a big pile of ketchup. But they do not understand romantic love.

"Why are guys always 'adjusting' themselves in public? (Sorry...I didn't know how else to say it!)"

—Colleen, 16; Hannah, 14; Maggie, 16; Cherline, 15; Ashely, 15; Jill, 14; Rosanna, 16

However, they certainly can experience romantic love. When I saw—and smelled—that boy in my kindergarten class, my heart pit-a-patted a little faster. My little palms got sticky with little girl sweat. My head felt a bit woozy. And my stomach did butterfly flips so strong that I was sure they could be seen on the outside of my clothing.

Yes, I fell in love.

I wondered what it would be like if he tried to sneak a kiss on the playground. (Never happened.) I wondered what it would be like if we sat down and actually talked to each other face to face. (Never happened.) I wondered what we would name the babies we'd buy at the baby hospital after we'd gotten married and moved into a cute little playhouse right next door to my mommy and daddy. (Never happened.)

Oh boy, was I in love.

And oh boy, was I clueless.

Falling in love is very real. There is actually a biological reaction that takes place in our bodies when we are attracted to someone. Hearts beat faster. Pupils dilate. Palms sweat. Brain chemicals do crazy things to the head

did you know... On average a human swallows seven spiders in a lifetime. **?**

and stomach. "Falling in love" is a very real and physical sensation.

Girls are very drawn to the emotional aspect of falling in love. For them love is about relationship, friendship, closeness, togetherness, and connectedness. Guys, on the other hand—especially during puberty and adolescence—are much more drawn to the physical aspect of love. That's not to say that guys don't care about girls as people and individuals. But the fact is, because of a guy's design and biology, he reacts to a girl in a very different way than the girl reacts to him.

"Why can't guys keep their hands off girls?"

—Louisa, 14

When a guy hits puberty, he is literally flooded with hormones. Every day testosterone washes through a guy's brain and body between five and seven times. When that happens, all the effects of testosterone are magnified and multiplied: competitive spirit, physical activity, energy, aggression, strength, sexual drive. It's not as though a guy morphs before your very eyes when the testosterone level rises. The effects aren't that openly obvious. I doubt that you'd be able to walk through a junior or senior high school and point out the guys who are experiencing a rush of testosterone at any given moment.

"It's hard being a guy because we have to deal with all the temptations and lust that come with being attracted to most girls and because television ads try to appeal to the sexual part of guys."

—A.J., 18

did you know...

If the small intestine were stretched out, it would be 22 feet long.

?

However, the effects of testosterone are very real. And in terms of sex drive those effects go a long way toward defining adolescence for guys.

Many girls surveyed expressed their frustration, confusion, and sometimes even disgust when it comes to teen guys and their attitude toward sex. But understanding what a guy experiences during puberty will go a long way towards understanding guys themselves.

Guys, you may remember, are between one and two years behind teen girls in terms of intellectual and emotional maturity. Their bodies, however, have already kicked into high gear. So a guy is in a position of having physical urges that he isn't ready to deal with emotionally or intellectually. That's why guys sometimes do and say crazy things around girls. In some ways it's true that teen guys are boys living in men's bodies.

"Why do guys always flirt?"

—Liz, 15

So the first thing you need to understand is that guys are at the mercy of testosterone surges that hit them without any warning and that create in them desires and urges that they don't always know how to deal with.

The other thing you need to know is that guys are very visual. While a girl is often motivated by what she feels, a guy is often motivated by what he sees. After all, Hooters is a thriving restaurant chain, but you don't see the male waiters at Red Lobster® decked out like strippers. Why? Guys love looking at women's bodies much more than girls love looking at guy's bodies.

did you know... The average person releases nearly a pint of intestinal gas by flatulence every day. Most is due to swallowed air. **?**

Which isn't to say that girls don't look at guys.

Just check out the teen girl magazines on the news rack. They're full of headlines like, "Photos of the 10 Hottest Teen Guys," "Who's the Cutest Guy on TV Today?" "Why We Like Buff and Brawn," and more. Girls look at guys. They look when they're at the beach. They look when they're reading magazines. They look when they're watching TV. They look when they're in school. But there are two big differences in the ways girls and guys look.

"Why do guys think sex is so important?"

— Jenna, 17

Girls have much better peripheral vision than guys do, so a girl can look at a guy without anyone ever knowing. Guys, on the other hand, usually look straight at the object that's caught their attention. So at the beach if a guy looks at a girl, everyone knows it. If a girl looks at a guy, it might be a secret to everyone around her.

Secondly, when a guy looks at a girl, it's often a basic biological response. He sees a girl. He looks. He admires. And sometimes his thoughts wander too far, and he moves beyond admiring to fantasizing and imagining. When that happens, a guy has moved from acceptable physical admiration to unacceptable physical lust.

Girls lust too. When a girl looks at a guy, it might initially be based on physical admiration and attraction. But sometimes her thoughts wander too far, and she begins to imagine what it would be like if the guy liked her, if he fulfilled her emotionally, if he spoke kind words to her and desired her and chose her to be his. When that happens, a

Ants don't burp.

?

girl has moved from acceptable physical admiration to unacceptable emotional lust (usually referred to as envy).

Lots of guys lust after girls.

And lots of girls lust after knowing that the guys lust after them.

"I don't like that guys are thought of as only thinking about sex."

—Drew, 17

Guys and girls alike are guilty of lust, but the roots of that lust are different based on their biology and design. As God designed it originally, a man's physical desire for a woman would result in commitment, physical intimacy, and a desire to care for and cherish her for the rest of his life. And a woman's desire for a man would result in commitment, physical intimacy, emotional connection, and a desire to know and bond with him for the rest of her life.

But the world has twisted many of God's good gifts, and sex has been twisted too.

"The hardest thing about being a guy is dealing with lust and trying to control your thought life."

— Justin, 18

Here are a few things that I want you to think about.

First, because guys are visually stimulated, you must be very wise and careful about how you clothe yourself. Often the girls who complain the loudest about the way guys look at them are the girls who are dressed in the skimpiest, most revealing, and most sexually suggestive clothing.

Does that mean you need to wear long skirts and frumpy, high-necked blouses for the rest of your life? No.

But it does mean you must try to think about things from a guy's perspective. A good rule of thumb is not to wear clothing that breaks what is sometimes called the "Three B" rule. That is, your clothing should never reveal any part of your breasts, your belly, or your butt. In today's fashion scene that can be challenging. A lot of shirts only cover part of a girl's midriff. A lot of shirts are cut low enough so that at least a certain amount of cleavage is revealed. And a lot of pants and shorts are cut so low at the waist that they barely cover what needs to be covered.

"Staying pure in today's world isn't easy."

—Justin, 19

Girls, if you want guys to look at you respectfully, then you need to dress respectfully. If you want guys to look at you as a person and not as an object, then you need to dress accordingly. Your clothes need to tell the truth about you. If you wear clothes that allow a guy to let his imagination run wild but then complain that he's not treating you as you deserve, you need to know that it's because you choose to wear clothes that lie about you. You wore clothes that said the opposite of what you truly desire. NOTE, HOWEVER, THAT NO MATTER WHAT YOU'RE WEARING, THAT'S NEVER AN EXCUSE FOR INAPPROPRIATE CONTACT, SEXUAL HARASSMENT, OR DATE RAPE.

"The influence of girls' skimpy clothing is hard to deal with."

—Michael, 13

did you know...

Humans use only 10 percent of their brains.

?

Also, you need to realize that a guy who looks at a girl is not necessarily thinking about her lustfully. There's a big difference between lust and admiration, between sinful desire and innocent appreciation. You won't always be able to tell what a guy is thinking. In fact, guys aren't always sure what their real motivation is either. But you must not necessarily assume that a guy who looks at you is thinking impure thoughts.

> "The hardest thing about being a guy is dealing with hormones."
>
> —Nick, 15

Here's the second thing you need to keep in mind. Because guys are faced with sexual urges that are often unexpected both in terms of when they strike and how strong they are, you need to protect both yourself and guys from any situations that might invite or encourage impure behavior. You must never lead a guy on or tease him with your actions, your words, or your clothes. You must never let a guy try to equate sex and love. Nor must you ever equate the two. Otherwise, you are at risk for finding yourself in one of the most unfortunate situations in a teen's life: that of being a girl who gives sex in order to get love or being with a guy who gives love in order to get sex.

I firmly believe that a guy and girl should never allow themselves to be in a situation that has the potential to create an atmosphere in which temptation could win out over wise decisions. In other words, a guy and girl should never be in a bedroom alone. They shouldn't even be at a house together if no one else is home. Dates should always be in public places, like restaurants, parks, bowling alleys, and miniature golf courses. If you are going somewhere with a guy, and either you or he is driving, you should contact your parents when you've arrived at your destination, and you should call them when you're leaving so that they know when to expect you home.

All of this might sound ridiculously old-fashioned to you, but God places an extraordinarily high value on purity . . . in all areas of a person's life. Purity isn't just about sexuality. It's also about how you talk to people. It's about how you think. It's about how you spend your money. It's about what kind of books you read and what kind of movies you watch.

"The hardest thing about being a guy is when girls dress and act scandalously. There's always been a problem with lust for guys, but the girls of today aren't doing anything to help us with the way they're dressing."

—Josh, 17

God calls us to live lives in which there is not even a hint of sexual immorality. That means he wants you to be careful not just about your actions, but also about how your actions might be interpreted by other people. If you have a really close guy friend for whom you have no romantic feelings, and if he feels the same way about you, it might seem fine to spend a lot of time alone together. What's the harm?

It is fine to spend time together; but alone time—just the two of you in a private place where no one can see you—isn't such a good idea. The day might possibly arrive when you and he are hanging out together alone, and you

A male moth can smell a female moth from 100 yards away. **?**

or he or both of you unexpectedly notice your feelings changing. Now you're in a compromising situation—romantic feelings, solitude, and no one to hold you accountable. Or maybe you're hanging out together alone, and your feelings toward each other don't change, but someone interprets your closeness and your constant private togetherness as something more than it really is. Now you're in what looks like a compromising situation, even though it really isn't, and you're in a position of having to defend and explain yourself. This is one of the reasons the Bible advises us to avoid situations that have even the appearance of a "hint of sexual immorality." I think it's awesome when girls and guys can be friends. They each have unique strengths and abilities they can bring to the relationship. A guy might feel safe talking to a girl about his emotions because he knows she probably understands about his feelings, and she won't laugh at or ridicule him. A girl might feel safe talking to a guy because she knows he's probably not going to share her thoughts and feelings with all of his friends.

> "I wish girls understood the pressure guys feel when dealing with girls and their fear of rejection."
>
> —Scott, 17

Or a girl who doesn't enjoy talking with friends might find that a guy friend offers what she needs—the opportunity to be friends without all the conversation and all the analyzing. A guy who isn't very competitive might find that a girl friend offers what he needs—the chance to be himself without having to prove he's more capable, funnier, or better than the next guy.

Many girls know that some guys act differently as soon as their other guy friends show up. All of a sudden the need to compete and the need to appear macho kick in, and the guy who a moment ago was caring and kind and talkative and friendly is now aloof and distant and swaggering. This is all part of growing up. Guys struggle with the desire to appear manly around their friends on the one hand and the desire to take off the tough guy mask when they have the chance. The guy friend still cares about you. He still likes you. He's just not quite mature enough yet to balance who he really is with who he feels he needs to be. But that will happen in time.

There are all kinds of reasons that friendships between guys and girls can be great. But underneath it all you must remember that teen guys are dealing with very high levels of testosterone that produce strong and unpredictable sexual urges. This is normal. This is the way God designed them. But in today's world that is full of sexual innuendo everywhere a person turns, you must be careful not to add more fuel to the fire. You need to protect both yourself and the guys you know by being wise, being aware, being cautious, and being committed to living a pure life.

"It's hard to be a guy and deal with lust."

—Daniel, 16; Bradford, 16; Matt, 19; Erik, 17

TO READ—

Ephesians 5:1-7

Genesis 39:6-12

TO THINK ABOUT—

1. Do girls bear any responsibility for helping guys fight against lust and temptation? Why, or why not?

2. Is there anything you need to change in the way you dress, act, or talk around guys?

3. How do you protect yourself from all the sexual messages that fill today's world, especially in the media?

4. How would you define "purity"? How do you think God defines "purity"?

GUYS WISH
GIRLS UNDERSTOOD . . .

(Top answer—how we think)

That guys just want to be immature sometimes.
—Mike, 17

The pressure guys feel when asking out girls
and the fear of rejection.
—Scott, 17

That we are sensitive people, too.
—Ben, 17

That we don't care as much about intricate details.
—Erik, 18

That just because we don't want to talk
doesn't mean we're mad.
—Daniel, 18

That they have a big effect on our self-esteem
and they shouldn't abuse that influence.
—Joe, 19

Our obsession with sweet cars.
—Josh, 18

That sports are important to us.
—Robby, 11

That we hate going
to our little sisters' tea parties.
—Aaron, 14

That we are not so emotional.
—Eric, 13

That we have to play paintball. I can't live without it.
—Joey, 13

That we're not all the same and we can change.
—Jacob, 12

That we don't care just about looks.
—Nathaniel, 13

That we are not dorks.
—Chase, 12

That we are very nice.
—Evan, 15

That we have feelings, too.
—James, 15

That we don't always play video games.
—Peter, 18

Me.

Chapter 10

Senior Knights of the Round Table

According to Mother Goose . . .

> *Snakes and snails and puppy dogs' tails*
> *That's what little boys are made of.*

But it would probably be more accurate to say . . .

> *Biology, brains, and rugged terrains*
> *That's what little boys are made of.*

Understanding how a guy's brain works goes a long way toward understanding guys themselves. Understanding how a guy's biology determines the onset of puberty and hormone levels goes a long way towards understanding guys themselves. And understanding the rugged terrain that a guy faces in today's world—"Be a man!" "Be tough!" "Don't be afraid to cry!" "Never let them see you sweat!"

did you know... Girls' hair is about half the diameter of guys' hair. **?**

"Pour out your feelings!"—goes a long ways toward understanding guys themselves.

But perhaps the best way of all to understand guys is to let guys do the talking, so I asked eight senior guys if they'd be willing to sit down and talk about a guy's life. They weren't overly enthusiastic at first, but when I offered free pizza, they happily agreed. Perhaps there is a little bit of truth to the old saying, "The way to a man's heart is through his stomach."

On a Tuesday night in May just a few days before their graduation, Kyle Anderson, Nate Benson, Ryan Bridgeman, Will Frank, Mike Frankberg, Mark Kozitka, Sam Mosher, and Adam Schmidt met me at the Young Life office for what I refer to as a meeting of the Senior Knights of the Round Table. (The table was actually square, but oh well.)

I invited these specific eight guys for several reasons. First, I'd known them for several years and had watched them grow from wiggly, squirrelly, crazy freshman boys into kind, decent, strong young men. Second, I admired their achievements academically, athletically, and artistically. Between the eight of them they represented hard work, determination, and a willingness to make sacrifices in order to pursue their dreams. Third, they represented a wide cross-section of personalities, interests, and accomplishments. And fourth, I thought they'd be willing to openly and honestly talk about their lives as guys and to answer the many questions I'd received from girls.

I was right.

The Young Life office has a couple of foosball tables. The Senior Knights of the Round Table (from now on referred to as SKoRT) arrived before the pizza did, so while

During an average lifetime males will spend 3,350 hours removing 8.4 meters of stubble.

?

they waited for food, they started in on an intense game of foosball. First order of business? To lay down the rules, a very "guy" thing.

"Spin or no spin?" asked one SKoRT.

"Spinning. Definitely," answered another.

In true guy fashion they wanted the rules and boundaries clearly stated so that the competition could be fair, intense, and regulated.

After a few minutes of high-energy sport complete with yelling, cheering, arguing, and score-keeping, the food arrived, and we sat down to eat (the first and most important order of business) and talk (an unpleasant but necessary stipulation of the evening).

And this is what they said.

> **Me:** Many girls wonder about a guy's maturity level. They often say things like, "Guys are so immature. Guys think stupid things are funny. Guys need to grow up." What do you think about that?

> **SKoRT:** When guys act immature, it's usually just a way of trying to get attention. We do grow out of it eventually . . . we don't act as stupid now as we did when we were freshmen. But most guys never grow out of it completely, which is why we have relapses now and then. Even our dads, when they get together with their friends, still sometimes do weird, silly things. It's the way guys are. It's fun to be immature. Not all the time, of course. But it's a great way to relax and put aside all the pressures of being responsible, strong, and serious.

Me: Girls don't understand how guys' emotions work. Do they hide them? Do they ignore them? Do they even have them?

SKoRT: Of course we have emotions. Girls are always saying they want us to show our emotions, but when we do, they make fun of us. Every guy is different, and we all show our emotions differently. If a guy cries when he's younger, like in elementary school, he gets laughed at by other kids. That can stick with him so that as he gets older, he avoids crying in front of other people.

But we all cry sometimes. Lots of times, athletes, who are supposed to be these tough, unfeeling guys, will cry at their year-end banquets or after a big game. It's safe to cry in those situations. People consider that acceptable.

A lot depends on a guy's family. If his dad cries openly, then the guy might feel more comfortable with it. If his dad always says, "Be tough. Don't ever let anyone see you cry," then the guy will probably have inhibitions about crying in public.

When guys see older men cry, it's kind of shocking at first. Here are all these grown men who you assumed were unshakable, and they're openly showing their feelings. But that usually only happens when it's a really major event, like a funeral. That's pretty typical for guys. We have emotions, but we usually only show them when they're really intense. The little things don't seem to affect us as much as girls, so to them it might appear like we're unfeeling. But we're not.

We've all learned something about girls and their emotions. When we see a girl cry, our immediate reaction is to try to fix things. But we know better now. We know this makes girls mad. We don't necessarily know what we should do when a girl cries, but we definitely know what we shouldn't do.

Me: Many people consider anger to be the one emotion guys know how to express. How do you deal with anger?

SKoRT: Anger can actually be the hardest emotion for guys. Some of us are known as being funny and comical, so when we act angry, other people assume we're joking, which makes us angrier than before. We blow up with frustration, which confuses the people around us. It would be nice if, when we expressed our anger, people took us seriously so it could be dealt with right away.

The one thing about guys and anger is that we're pretty good at dealing with it and then letting it go. It seems to us like girls love the drama of dragging out their feelings as long as they can. We'd rather take a problem, solve it, then drop it. So when we're angry, we want to deal with it quickly and be done with it.

One of our friends played a practical joke on a guy we know—he let all the air out of the

The average human produces 25,000 quarts of spit in a lifetime.

?

guy's tires. The guy was really mad. He reamed out our friend royally . . . but then he was done with it.

In our opinion it's a bad idea for a guy to argue with a girl about things, even if she wants to, because girls often drag things out and make them last longer. They always analyze things to death and are still fuming long after we've let it go. Then they get mad at us for not still being mad about whatever the problem was in the first place.

Me: Girls don't understand the macho, tough guy act that so many guys seem to display. Where does that come from?

SKoRT: Most of that is just showing off. We grow out of it for the most part. There's pressure—maybe from TV and movies—to be like that, and so when we're younger, that's what we do. But as we get older and feel more confident in who we are, it's not such a big deal anymore.

Me: Girls consider themselves to be good conversationalists . . . except when it comes to guys. They get frustrated because, in their mind, guys never want to talk. Why is that?

SKoRT: We'd just rather do something than talk. Sitting around and talking isn't very exciting. Part of the problem can be finding a topic that interests everyone. Sometimes it's hard for us to put our thoughts into words clearly. And honestly, sometimes it's not enjoyable to talk to girls (it's not always unenjoyable . . . we all have girl friends we talk to, but since you asked . . .) because they drag everything out and talk so much. It can take some girls forever to tell a story that, for a guy, only needs a few sentences. That's not a bad thing, but that's probably part of the reason that we don't always want to sit down and have a conversation.

Me: One of the most asked questions by teen girls was, "Why do guys change when they're around their friends? We can be having a nice time together, but when their friends show up—boom!—it's like they become a different person."

SKoRT: For some of us it feels like guys live in two different worlds. We're supposed to be sensitive around girls but tough around our friends. Part of it is wanting to save face. We don't want our friends to see us acting soft or whipped around a girl. We don't want it to look like the girl is controlling us and our behavior.

But this changes as we get older. We don't care anymore if our friends see us having a conversation with a girl or hanging out with a girl. We really do become more sensitive as we get older, and if we'd known how much we hurt some girls' feelings when we were younger, we probably wouldn't have done a lot of the things we did.

Me: Girls really want to understand why guys are so competitive and why they are so fascinated with sports.

did you know...

Girls blink twice as much as guys.

?

SKoRT: So many of a boy's heroes are athletes. When we were in elementary school, there was this famous baseball player that we all looked up to and wanted to be like. Lots of boys are drawn to sports because of the famous athletes. For those of us who are involved in athletics, there is the adrenaline rush that a person gets right before competing and after winning. It's pretty amazing. That might be part of the whole sports fanatic thing too.

But we're not all athletic, and we're not all into sports. Those of us who aren't used to get teased about it all the time. We'd get called "girl" and "wimp." When guys are younger, there's an idea that only the athletes are cool. But we know that's not true. We're all pretty happy with who we are, and that's a result of being older and more mature.

Me: Girls have this idea that all guys are really interested in sex and that they think about it all the time. Is that true? How do you deal with temptation and lust?

SKoRT: We do not think about it all the time. And when we do think about it, it isn't always a fantasy thing. Girls act like we sit around all day imagining what it's like to have sex, and we don't. Wondering about sex and thinking about it in a healthy way is not the same thing as actually doing it.

It's true that we look at girls. Some of that is just instinctive. Our heads turn when we notice a girl, and we don't even realize it's happening. When we look at a girl, it doesn't mean we like her or that we're undressing her with our eyes or that we're having lustful thoughts about her. Lots of times we're looking just because it's how we respond to what's around us.

We don't understand why girls get so upset about us looking at them. They're always saying things like, "He's so cute," which is kind of the same thing, but no one ever says, "All girls think about is what a guy looks like."

It doesn't help us that some girls dress the way they do. We are distracted by what we see very easily. When we see girls dress like that, we often wonder whether they just want attention, whether they hate their moms, and whether they respect themselves at all because it sure doesn't seem like they do. The way a girl dresses says a lot about her. Girls can dress nicely and attractively without looking like a prostitute. That doesn't impress a guy at all. He'll probably notice her and look at her, but that's not the kind of girl that most guys are interested in.

This is another maturity thing. As we've gotten older, we've learned that there are certain things we can do to protect ourselves. One of our friends is really tall, and he actually walks through the high school halls looking up at the ceiling because if he didn't, he'd have a perfect view right down the front of every girl's shirt.

He sometimes runs into stuff and looks like a total klutz, but what he's doing is really cool.

It's not always easy to take the high road, especially with all the influences around us. But it is possible to make the right decisions. Especially if girls and guys have the same goals and commitments.

There you have it. Straight answers right from the guys themselves. It probably doesn't clear up all your questions, but that's not really the point. The point is to begin respecting, honoring, and accepting guys for who they are, both as individuals and as an entire group.

Guys are awesome. God had a great idea when he created guys. And he had a great idea when he created girls. And when they view each other not as annoyances to be avoided or as problems to be fixed, then we will all be better off. After all, God said that his creation was very good only after he'd created both males and females. It's time for all of us to begin living as though we truly believed this.

TO READ—

1 John 4:7-21 (. . . all about God's love for all people, female and male alike . . .)

TO THINK ABOUT—

1. What new things have you learned about the differences between guys and girls?

2. Will the things you've learned change the way you view or react to or communicate with guys? How?

3. Now that you know the real differences between males and females, what do you think God's purpose was in creating these differences?

4. What are the biggest challenges guys and girls face in understanding and respecting one another?

P.P.S.

It all ended with a T-shirt.

Actually, it wasn't really a T-shirt. It was a T-shirt iron-on decal.

After spending months reading, researching, discussing, teaching, writing, and thinking about the issues that sometimes divide guys and girls, there was a very brief moment when I thought, "Maybe this really isn't such a big deal after all. Maybe girls really do understand guys. Maybe girls really do respect and honor guys. Maybe girls really do recognize that guys are a well-planned and dearly loved creation of God. Maybe girls really do give guys the benefit of the doubt in terms of their maturity level. Maybe girls really are nice and kind and decent and polite to guys . . . in which case this book isn't really necessary at all."

A hog's sweat glands are in its snout.

?

Just as all of these thoughts were racing through my head, I opened up one of the many teen girl magazines piled on my desk (research purposes only . . . I'll be glad to get rid of them when this is finished because even though I enjoy some of the articles and some of the information, a lot of the stuff in there about guys is ridiculous, and some of it is downright false), and out fell one of those annoying inserts that make it hard to flip through a magazine smoothly.

This particular insert was a free T-shirt iron-on decal that said—

GIRLS KICK BUTT.

The implication was that boys don't kick butt—in other words, that girls are better than boys.

And at that moment I knew that this topic of guys, girls, gender differences, and respect for one another needed to be addressed.

Girls, it's my hope that you'll walk away from this book with a newfound awe for God's creation of humanity—both male and female; that you'll understand a little bit more clearly how guys' brains and biology make them who they are; that you'll realize that "different" is not the same as "better" or "worse"; that you'll be more understanding of the pressures and struggles guys face; that, even when they annoy you, bug you, and tick you off, you'll remember that guys are human beings, not some subspecies to be looked down on and made fun of; and most of all that you'll have a newfound amazement for God, the one who imagined, designed, thought of, planned, and created every person who will ever walk on this earth.

did
you
know... A box turtle's gender is determined by the color of its eyes. **?**

He's awesome. Don't ever forget it. Loving him will help you love everyone around you . . . including guys.

—Crystal

SOURCES

The book you just read is full of facts, statistics, studies and quotes, all of which come from very reliable sources. If this were a textbook, it would be littered with footnotes. But this isn't a textbook, and who wants to read a book that's littered with footnotes anyway? We wanted this to be a fun, easy-to-read, truthful book, so instead of footnoting all the facts, statistics, studies, and quotes, we decided to list our sources at the end and leave it at that. That way you can check the information later if you want without being constantly interrupted while you read. Happy . . . and smooth . . . reading!

Science of the Sexes, Discovery Channel (available on DVD or VHS)

Bringing Up Boys, by James Dobson, Tyndale, 2001

Wild at Heart, by John Eldredge, Nelson, 2001

Teenage Boys!, by Bill Beausay, Waterbrook Press, 1998

You Just Don't Understand, by Deborah Tannen, Ph.D., Harper Collins, 1990

Boys and Girls Learn Differently!, by Michael Gurian and Patricia Henley, Jossey-Bass, 2001

The Wonder of Boys, by Michael Gurian, Tarcher/Putnam, 1996

A Return to Modesty, by Wendy Shalit, Touchstone, 1999

Why Men Don't Listen and Women Can't Read Maps, by Barbara and Allan Pease, Broadway Books, 1998

The Primal Teen, by Barbara Strauch, Doubleday, 2003

Why Men Don't Iron, by Anne and Bill Moir, Citadel Press, 1999

 did you know... In 205 b.c., the Romans passed a law prohibiting women from driving chariots. **?**